Self-Care

for

Black Men

100 Ways to Heal and Liberate

Jor-El Caraballo, LMHC

ADAMS MEDIA
NEW YORK   LONDON   TORONTO   SYDNEY   NEW DELHI

**adams**media

Adams Media
An Imprint of Simon & Schuster, Inc.
100 Technology Center Drive
Stoughton, Massachusetts 02072

Copyright © 2023 by Simon &
Schuster, Inc.

All rights reserved, including the right to
reproduce this book or portions thereof
in any form whatsoever. For information,
address Adams Media Subsidiary Rights
Department, 1230 Avenue of the
Americas, New York, NY 10020.

First Adams Media hardcover edition
November 2023

ADAMS MEDIA and colophon are
registered trademarks of Simon &
Schuster, Inc.

For information about special discounts
for bulk purchases, please contact Simon
& Schuster Special Sales at 1-866-506-
1949 or business@simonandschuster.com.

The Simon & Schuster Speakers Bureau
can bring authors to your live event. For
more information or to book an event,
contact the Simon & Schuster Speakers
Bureau at 1-866-248-3049 or visit our
website at www.simonspeakers.com.

Interior design by Michelle Kelly

Manufactured in the United States of
America

1 2023

Library of Congress Cataloging-in-
Publication Data
Names: Caraballo, Jor-El, author.
Title: Self-care for black men / Jor-El
Caraballo, LMHC.
Description: Stoughton, Massachusetts:
Adams Media, 2023. | Includes
bibliographical references and index.
Identifiers: LCCN 2023024296 |
ISBN 9781507221044 (hc) | ISBN
9781507221051 (ebook)
Subjects: LCSH: African-American
men--Mental health. | African
Americans--Health and hygiene.
Classification: LCC
RC451.5.B53 C37 2023 | DDC
613/.042308996073--dc23/
eng/20230705
LC record available at https://lccn.loc
.gov/2023024296

ISBN 978-1-5072-2104-4
ISBN 978-1-5072-2105-1 (ebook)

Many of the designations used by
manufacturers and sellers to distinguish
their products are claimed as trademarks.
Where those designations appear in
this book and Simon & Schuster, Inc.,
was aware of a trademark claim, the
designations have been printed with initial
capital letters.

Letter to the Reader

I'm glad that you're here. That you're reading this means that one of two things is true: You've realized you need to make time to take better care of yourself, or someone you love has cared enough to gift this book to you. Either way, it's a win-win!

Self-care is not a perfect journey. Different factors and barriers, including mental ones, get in the way of self-care. Even when armed with the right tools and education, you may still struggle to put some of the suggestions in this book into practice. Give yourself grace, but also hold yourself accountable. Looking after yourself can be difficult, but if you try new things, you will gain a lot. Your health will improve. Your relationships will get better. Your mental health will become more stable and secure.

Within these pages are opportunities to lean into ease and relaxation. There will be times when you will take a deeper look at yourself and at internalized perspectives on masculinity and Blackness. This might be uncomfortable, but being uncomfortable is necessary for growth. These challenges are offered in love and liberation. Have faith in your ability to do "the work." I have faith that there is some part of you that will do whatever you need to take better care of yourself. Be proud of yourself for starting here.

As a Black man and therapist, I know that the ways we heal may look different from the ways mainstream wellness talks about health. Black men experience the same challenges as anyone else, but with the added pressures of racism, increased stigma, and oppression. The path to healing is different and needs to take into account our lived realities and the complexity of contemporary Black masculinity. This book aims to provide space for exploring these ideas.

While you're here, I have one favor to ask. If any part of this book inspires you, heals you, or otherwise brings you to a new understanding, I want you to lend your copy to another Black man in your life (or purchase a copy for him as a gift). Help spread the word that Black men *need* and *deserve* to take care of themselves. Be generous in sharing insights and tips you gain from these pages so that the next person goes a little further along on his own journey of self-care. As they say, "Each one, teach one."

Your brother in care,
Jor-El Caraballo

Contents

Introduction. 11

Write in Your Journal. 13
Define Blackness for Yourself 15
Make That Therapy Appointment 17
Make a To-Do List. 19
Take a Moment to Breathe. 21
Stretch It Out. 23
Organize and Declutter Your (Work) Space 25
Create a Sanctuary at Home. 27
Try a Holistic Healer 29
Make That Doctor's Appointment 31
Rethink Your Relationship with Food. 33
Write an Unsent Letter. 35
Listen to Your Body 37
Take a Mindful Walk 39
Journal on Your Own Terms. 41
Try Floating 43
Allow Yourself to Feel. 45
Try a New Spiritual Practice. 47
Stop Responding When Someone Calls You "Bro"
    (Unless You're Okay with That). 49
Challenge Impostor Syndrome. 51
Debrief from Vicarious Trauma 53
Learn Your Toxic Traits. 55

Adjust Your Relationship with Anger and Rage 57
Lean Into Vulnerability 59
Take an Honest Look at Your Mental Health 61
Rethink the Strong Black Man Trope 63
Give Yourself Space to Cry 65
Practice Gratitude with the G.L.A.D. Technique 67
Take a Depression Screener 69
Reexamine Your Relationship with Your Body 71
Acknowledge an Act of Resistance 73
Build Community with Your LGBTQIA+ Family 75
Communicate Assertively 77
Reflect On Your Highs and Lows 79
Check Your Gas Tank 81
Develop a Sleep Routine 83
Set Weekly Intentions 85
Try a Worry Dump 87
Read Something New 89
Adjust Your Negative Thoughts 91
Practice Daily Grooming 93
Make Amends 95
Reach Out to a Friend 97
Respond to a Microaggression 99
Try Meditation 101
Set a Boundary 103
Limit Your Alcohol Intake 105
Make SMART Goals 107
Make an Active Coping Plan 109
Take a Nap 111
Embrace Your Softness 113

Revisit a Dream Deferred 115
Heal a Father Wound 117
Get to Know Your Shadow 119
Engage In Meaning-Making 121
Take a Trip (Maybe Even Solo) 123
Take Yourself on a Date 125
Permit Yourself to Grieve 127
Try Forest Bathing 129
Create a Vision Board for Your Career 131
Conceptualize a Feeling 133
Take a Mental Health Day from Work 135
Express What You're Feeling 137
Spend Time with a Pet 139
Reflect On Your Experiences with Anti-Black Racism 141
Read to Reduce Stress and Anxiety 143
Change Your Perspective 145
Lean Into the Power of Collective Healing 147
Visit with Your Ancestors 149
Practice Radical Hope 151
Connect to Your Inner Child 153
Embrace the Wise Mind for Decision-Making 155
Identify and Name White Mediocrity 157
Find Your Safe Space 159
Make a Positivity Playlist 161
Develop Your Spiritual Self 163
Get a Massage 165
Write Your Own Obituary 167
Clarify Your Personal Values 169
Address a Mother Wound 171

Limit Your Time on Social Media. 173
Embrace Racial Pride Through History 175
Heal Through Dance 177
Personalize Your Environment 179
Acknowledge Your Weak Points 181
Cope with Sexual Dysfunction. 183
Reflect On Your Positive Qualities 185
Get Real about Colorism 187
Learn More about Mental Health and Mental Illness 189
Ask for Help. 191
Embody Radical Acceptance 193
Explore Music Therapy. 195
Foster a Good Relationship with Finances 197
Start an Exercise Routine 199
Take Care of Your Sexual Health 201
Become a Critical Consumer of Media. 203
Participate and Invest in Your Community. 205
Prepare a Special Meal for Yourself. 207
Release Familial Burdens 209
Practice and Embrace Joy. 211

Further Reading. 213
Acknowledgments 215
Index 217

Introduction

Black men deserve restoration. We deserve to do the things that help us operate as the best versions of ourselves every day. But what do these things look like in today's world? How do you take care of your mental health when men who look like you frequently die at the hands of the police? How can you make room for joy when you have so much on your to-do list? How do you cultivate peace and refuge when you're not sure how to address your needs? How do you navigate a challenging workplace? What strategies can help you strengthen your mental health and wellness to become a healthier father, friend, or partner?

In *Self-Care for Black Men*, you will find the answers to these questions in the form of self-care. More than exercising just for the sake of it, or getting sleep when you need it, self-care is a way of nourishing your body, mind, and spirit and resisting the systems of inequality that try to keep you down. Each of the one hundred entries in this book provides important background and context for Black men regarding a specific self-care practice and offers easy steps for putting that practice into action. You will:

- Find the strategies that help you live a balanced life on a daily basis, like making a mental health coping plan.
- Reject beliefs wrapped in internalized colonial ideas and embrace healing-centered justice, like embodying radical acceptance.

- Unpack cultural programming to embrace self-determination and self-definition, like clarifying your personal values.
- Release trauma and reframe thought patterns that cause distress, like addressing a mother wound.
- Recognize the importance of relationship building and community care, like reaching out to a friend and practicing healing in community.

You may read a new entry and take a new action daily or weekly, or focus on multiple actions in a week or month, depending on what feels right for you. You may decide to read the entries in order, or skip around based on what's most relevant to your life. However you approach this book, *Self-Care for Black Men* offers both practical advice and inspiration for building a self-care plan based on *your* needs.

This is your opportunity to take your mental, physical, and spiritual health firmly within your own hands. It is your chance to fight back against the challenges and oppression sent your way—through the power of self-care.

Write in Your Journal

I've been a therapist long enough to know that "writing in your journal" is almost a mental health cliché at this point. I've also had my fair share of clients laugh at the suggestion, and I don't take it personally. In large part, there's a misunderstanding of what journaling is or what it needs to be. This creates a lot of pressure to do it the "right way"—so much so that you focus on the process rather than benefiting from the experience overall. I'll share some insight here into why it can be a helpful part of your self-care routine. This is important to understand because Black men have not been encouraged to be articulate about their feelings and experiences.

In American culture, men tend to struggle with two things: having the language to express themselves and connecting to their emotions more deeply in general. These struggles are something that you've probably experienced yourself if you've had trouble sorting through an argument with a friend or romantic partner, only to find yourself frustrated and worn down at the end. Sound familiar? This is a common challenge for Black men who conform to the trope that they are more about action than articulation.

But as society continues to shift, there is more pressure than ever for Black men to dig deeper with their emotions and discuss their concerns and vulnerabilities with the people who care about them.

The reason therapists often suggest journaling as a tool in managing mental health is that it engages a different level of processing than just thinking about your thoughts alone. Think about it this way: We spend the entirety of our lives in our heads with our thoughts, but rarely do we fully see and comprehend what we're thinking and feeling. Odds are you rarely stop to think about and reflect on how you're feeling. However, reflection in written form forces you to review those thoughts and feelings and see them with greater intensity and clarity. This often happens in therapy when I repeat something a client has said verbatim. They are usually shocked at how emotional that reflection makes them feel.

This experience happens when you spend time journaling. You can more fully process what you are thinking and feeling. Being able to connect to thoughts and feelings is more meaningful than you may think.

Take Action

Take a piece of paper (or open up a notes app on your phone) and write down five adjectives that describe your day. Try to stay away from overused words like "good" and "okay." Once you've written them down, stop and look at them together. Do they capture your day fully? If not, you may need a bit more time to reflect. For some people, it's also easier to write out full phrases or sentences. If you find it hard to find the right words, then you can also use a feelings wheel, dictionary, or thesaurus for more inspiration and nuance. Use these techniques anytime you want to journal. Over time, you will build a broader emotional vocabulary for your own insight, which will also help you communicate with clarity to others.

Define Blackness for Yourself

What does it mean to be Black? There are millions of Black people across the many countries and cultures in the African Diaspora, and you will likely find as many definitions or interpretations of Blackness. Have you stopped to consider what your definition is and how that sense of identity is shaped by your immediate environment?

As children, we learn a great deal about ourselves through observation and modeling. If you grew up with Black parents and Black family members, those people in your life are likely your biggest models of what it means to be Black. If you are Black and grew up in a non-Black family as the adopted son or daughter of parents of a different race, your experience and identification with Blackness likely came from outside of your home.

One of the tropes related to Blackness contends that "Black men don't go to therapy! That's white people stuff." You may have heard or even said something similar to this. Sometimes it's good-natured humor and fun. At other times, you can feel the weight of those messages as someone tries to keep you in line with how they see Blackness. And, if you fall outside of those lines, you can be ridiculed, or even socially excluded, for not falling into these so-called social norms.

There are many different perspectives on how to identify and describe Blackness as an identity. Black Caribbeans tend to see themselves as different from Black Americans, who see themselves as different from Black Africans, and so forth. This idea probably isn't new to you. Neither is the idea of disconnectedness and isolation you may have felt as a result of these kinds of obstacles to creating a more cohesive diaspora (the movement away from homelands).

If you don't fall within the socially acceptable limits of Blackness, you may feel isolated from others. Sometimes, that disconnection can be so painful that people will identify with other people. Consider what the notorious O.J. Simpson once said: "I'm not Black, I'm O.J." This is a perfect example. Those kinds of statements speak to a deeper rift between community and self. Maybe you have felt that disconnection in certain conversations involving within-group racial policing too. It's just one of many residuals of the intergenerational trauma of slavery that forced our ancestors to disassociate from Africa. Colorism within Black communities is another residual.

Take Action

Today I want you to permit yourself to define Blackness on your own terms. Does that mean you allow yourself to proclaim your love for country music? What about your distaste for current rap culture? Maybe it means permitting yourself to connect with your African roots, or perhaps that's not all that important to you personally. There's no judgment here. Take a moment to write down some words that reflect your personal experience of Blackness and what you want to embody.

Make That Therapy Appointment

If you've been thinking about starting therapy, this is your sign to send that email and request an appointment.

Historically, the words "Black men" and "therapy" have rarely been part of the same sentence. But psychotherapy, or talk therapy with a trained mental health provider, is helpful whether you are looking to make a career switch or trying to manage symptoms related to challenges such as depression or bipolar disorder. It runs the gamut in terms of the kind of support it can offer.

Unfortunately, one belief you've internalized to some degree is that seeking help is a sign of a man's weakness. This almost seems to be coded in the DNA of the modern Black man. Thankfully, in recent years, the tide has been shifting; more Black men are understanding the importance of mental health and the value of therapy. Black men can thank Black women for courageously opening the door for us. Specifically, as Black women continue to normalize the notion of getting support, more and more Black men are following their example by seeking therapy. After all, Black women navigate the world through double marginalization based on race *and* gender. While it is not the only place to get support, a therapist's office is a safe space to address anxieties related to discrimination. A good therapist can also help identify any past mental health misdiagnosis.

It's okay for you to need help. We all need help sometimes.

Take Action

If you've already identified a therapist (or two) who might help you, send that email or make that call today. Do it right now. It takes less than five minutes. Keep it simple and short. There's no need to put off feeling better any longer. You deserve peace of mind. If you haven't identified options yet, set aside maybe a half hour or so to do some Internet research on providers in your area. You could also ask friends and relatives to make queries within their networks to help you identify therapists who could support you. There is no time like the present to get started.

Make a To-Do List

Mental organization is an often-overlooked aspect of mental health. This is the case because most of us occasionally reach situational limits, periods when our brain can only process and organize so much. Once it's overloaded with information, other stressors, and mental health concerns, the brain doesn't work as efficiently. Think of it as your web browser with too many tabs open. Music is playing and you have no idea which tab it's coming from. This is your brain on stress. For Black men, some of those open tabs are personal life circumstances, such as work or family life, and this compounds with external forces like discrimination that continuously run in the back of your mind.

Have you ever made a health appointment only to arrive at the appointment at the wrong time or on the wrong day? Do you have a habit of misplacing items at home or work? Do you struggle with doing the things you know you need to get done? If you've answered "yes" to any of these questions, you might be dealing with reduced cognitive performance.

This isn't necessarily a cause for alarm, but it is important to recognize that these kinds of mistakes are often early signs that you are not at your best. Forgetting an appointment or an errand you were supposed to do is a sign that your mental focus is split and your brain is trying to keep up with too much. It means you're probably operating beyond your current capacity. When that happens, it is easy to be forgetful and misplace things.

Using organizational tools such as a to-do list is an incredibly helpful way to navigate a busy life with multiple responsibilities. If paper and pen are not your thing, you can easily use a smartphone or other technology that prompts you to do tasks with an alarm or a reminder message for a certain time and/or location. If you add reminders to your to-do list, you can reduce your cognitive load. Wouldn't that make life a little easier?

Take Action

Your task here is simple: Figure out what method of reminders is most likely to guarantee you success. As I sometimes tell clients, this is not the time to play games with yourself and think about what you "should" use to be organized. I'm a fan of whatever works! Whether it's a daily written agenda, an electronic calendar, or a reminders app, use the tool that will work best for you—one that you'll actually use.

One other thing to keep in mind is that it's also important to have some patience with yourself because it might take a few different tries to determine what to-do method works best for you. If you run into any speed bumps as you try to figure out what system works best for you, slow down, roll with it, and pivot when there's a need.

Take a Moment to Breathe

"I can't breathe."

Those were the final words of Eric Garner when he was killed at the hands of the NYPD in 2014. Even long before that moment, Black men have been acutely aware of the fear of meeting the same fate.

This kind of tragedy and trauma is not new to us due to generational lineages storied with lynching and public death at the hands of people in power. You have likely feared the day that you (or another brother you love) could follow the same destiny. The fear is born out of the vicarious trauma of seeing people who look, sound, and maybe even act like you die at the hands of those who are supposed to "protect and serve." This has changed our own experience with breath.

This kind of racial stress and vicarious trauma exists within the body—creating a deep, internal tension that prevents you from being truly at rest. Your breath—the thing you long to protect—ironically becomes trapped in your chest and the shallowness of your fear. Take a moment to think about it right now: When was the last time you took a full, deep breath and felt relaxed?

While shallow breathing can clue you in to your body's ongoing anxiety and fear, it can also help call in relaxation and ease. This is because your breath is directly connected to your fight-or-flight response. When you are scared or anxious, breathing shallows and quickens as your sympathetic nervous system activates. When you are in a state of relaxation, breathing slows and becomes fuller and deeper as your parasympathetic nervous system takes over. Because of this, you can intentionally use your breath to soothe your nervous system with simple intentional breathing exercises.

Take Action

One of my favorite breathing exercises is called box breathing. This exercise has reportedly been used by Navy SEALs and by snipers for promoting relaxation to help them do their jobs effectively. You are using it for more peaceful reasons here. It's a simple, yet effective strategy to help regulate your nervous system and engage in the relaxation function of your brain.

First, you will breathe in (inhale) for four seconds. Then you hold that breath for four more seconds. Next, you breathe out (exhale) for four seconds. Then you hold for four more seconds with empty lungs. Repeat the cycle over again with a new inhale. To help you focus on the breathing, you can trace a box with your finger during this exercise. Draw one line of the box with each inhale and each exhale. You can do as many of these sixteen-second cycles as you like until you feel relaxed.

Stretch It Out

"Mental health is as important as physical health." People who say this may have good intentions, but mental health and physical health are actually intertwined in what is called the mind-body connection. Examples include the fact that exercise, or lack of it, impacts mental health. Nutritional psychiatry has also emerged as a way to treat mental illness because of the brain's relationship to gut microbiome (the delicate balance between microorganisms such as bacteria in your gastrointestinal system, which impacts your mood).

In addition, some conditions such as anxiety and depression—particularly for Black folks—are more likely to create physical symptoms in a process called somatization. For example, stress can cause some people to develop headaches, chest pain, nausea, or fatigue. If you pay attention, these are often early signs you need to address your mental health.

Stretching regularly can help reduce muscle tension, fatigue, and stiffness. It enables muscles in the body to become lubricated, allowing for a greater range of motion and ease. When you are in a constant state of physical tension, your body may also send the message back to your brain that you have something to be tense about. This can create an unintentional and ongoing cycle of discomfort and distress.

The kind of relief you get from moving your body is powerful. I understand that attending yoga, gym, or Pilates sessions may not feel entirely comfortable for many Black men who believe African-American males don't exist in those spaces. If you don't like to visit the gym or other workout venues, stretching is something you can do in just a few minutes per day. You don't need to take up yoga to stretch. You don't need to be a Pilates master or a yogi, because stretching isn't complicated. It is something you can do at a place and time of your choosing, even for just a few minutes. Will you give yourself permission to honor your body and your mind in this simple way?

Take Action

Take a few moments to get into some stretching. If you're sitting at your desk, stand up and reach toward the sky and then reach down and try to touch your toes. If you have difficulty with mobility, you can also do some neck or facial stretches. For example, roll your neck from side to side. Do whatever you can to get the juices flowing. Also, don't forget to be patient and consistent in your stretching regimen. Your body and mind will feel the impact over time.

Organize and Declutter
Your (Work) Space

As a result of flex practices adopted in the wake of the COVID-19 pandemic, many of us are now working full-time from home or are splitting our work time between home and office. This means you have less direct in-office supervision. It also means there is a greater likelihood that you will make organizational errors or lose focus because you're struggling as you sift through work-related clutter. Those situations are not good for your mental health. Black men face a lot of external and internalized pressure at work. Staying organized can help you manage the stress within your immediate control and help you stay more productive throughout your work day.

You may not know this, but your workspace (or living space) reflects your internal psychological space. Have you discovered that when you aren't doing well mentally, your work or living space often looks a bit messier? Conversely, have you ever noticed how you feel your best when your space is clutter-free with everything in its place? That's not an accident.

It indicates that the surrounding physical space is often a reflection of how you are thinking and feeling. While this isn't quite a diagnostic tool, a person's living space is often an indicator of how that person is doing internally.

Aside from the barrier of being busy, it's common for those living with conditions such as depression and chronic anxiety to have difficulty keeping their personal living spaces cleaned and organized. Why is that? In my experience, it's hard to focus on the straightforward activities of daily life when your mental health concerns demand so much of your energy and attention.

Even if you're not struggling with a mental illness, your space can still reflect how well you are organized and grounded. This is something I have even observed in my personal space: If things get too cluttered, or if it's been a while since I've organized, it's highly likely that I'm being pulled in too many directions.

Is the same true for you?

Take Action

Take a minute to think about the organizational state of your personal space. If you are at your desk or in your home, look around and ask yourself, "Am I comfortable with how this place looks right now? Does this space help me feel peaceful, productive, or at ease?" If not, take five minutes right now to clean and organize a small section. For example, you can clear off a coffee table, remove napkins from the dining table, or put those used cups from your desk in the sink for washing. Start small and tackle little zones a few minutes at a time, especially if you've struggled to maintain a clean and organized space in the past. You will get to see the results of your efforts quickly, and you can build on that momentum to transform your space over time.

Create a Sanctuary at Home

A home can be more than just a place where you lay your head. It can be a space meant for rest and rejuvenation. However, all too often, Black men are not intentional about creating that kind of space for themselves. Sometimes it's because we don't understand how our immediate environment makes us feel. This is, in large part, because many Black men hold the traditional perspective that the home is somehow a woman's domain. There's nothing wrong with that perspective if it works for you and your family. However, when Black men encounter race-based physical and psychological threats in the outside world, it is even more important to have a place of refuge inside the home.

Have you ever entered a space and immediately found it to be soothing? Conversely, have you ever walked into a room and immediately got the sense that it was too formal or stuffy for you? Environments have an impact, both positively and negatively, on your mental health. A whole area of research (environmental health) explores these kinds of concerns. And while no one can feel comfortable 100 percent of the time, why not try to cultivate space within your home that helps you feel the way you'd like to feel?

It may take some time to figure out what makes you feel most at ease. Is that sitting in front of the TV in a quiet room, or are you more at ease in a meditation/wellness space where you sit and breathe or do yoga? Is there a kind of lighting that hurts your eyes? Are there scents that help you feel calm? This is all information you can use to curate a space at home that enables you to retain or restore your mental health. There's no right or wrong way to create a space of peace for you. If you've long ignored your emotional and physiological need for ease, this is your opportunity to be active in your healing.

Take Action

Identify a physical space in your home where you can find rest and refuge. This space can be an entire room or it can be a corner of a room that you design. The space could include furniture and things that help you feel at ease and comfortable. Is this your man cave covered in sports memorabilia? Could this be your private study with space for work and/or a corner for naps and rest? This is your space to rest and shed the stresses of any day. Take some time to develop a vision and bring it to reality.

Try a Holistic Healer

How comfortable are you with taking care of your physical self? I'm imagining that you've found this book in your quest for a more active self-care process. I'm glad that you're here! Black men don't take enough time to take care of themselves. As you explore more options for intentional self-care, you may find that you need professional help with achieving a sense of peace. For example, you might consider seeking out holistic healers.

Due to pressures such as discrimination in the workplace, social anxieties, and ongoing physical threats to Black safety, Black men need much more support than they are collectively getting. *You* need space and time to heal from all the stressors you encounter daily. Most men believe they handle these pressures well, and there may be some truth to that. However, even with some coping skills, you must consider that the rates of chronic health issues such as heart disease and high blood pressure are higher among Black people—especially Black men—because of racial stressors. You can do all that you can daily to power through and stay focused on your goals, but the research is clear that all these things take a bigger toll on our minds and bodies than anyone would like to think.

When it comes to taking care of your mental, spiritual, and physical health, there are many service options and providers to consider. You could consult a doctor or a host of other health practitioners who can teach you different ways to take care of yourself. Yoga practitioners can help with physical and spiritual alignment. Reiki healers work with moving energy and healing. Acupuncturists help manage qi (the body's natural energy). Nutritionists provide dietary consultation. Chiropractors help with physical realignment. Health coaches can help you reach fitness and nutrition goals. Holistic healing is dedicated to treating the whole person—mind, body, and spirit. Holistic providers use their expertise to help you achieve overall health and optimal wellness.

It can be helpful to step outside of your comfort zone and try something new. There are always opportunities to learn from different cultures and new sources of knowledge. In addition to experiencing health benefits, you may also expose yourself to new perspectives that could enable you to deal more effectively with life's challenges.

Take Action

Holistic healers come in all sorts of varieties, and many healer options are available to support your health goals. Start by doing some research on holistic remedies for any concerns you might have—whether it's trying to deal with stress or learning more about the diet that best fits your lifestyle. Step outside of your comfort zone and schedule a consultation with a provider who can help you take care of yourself. We all need a little help sometimes.

Make That Doctor's Appointment

Black men, historically, have a *terrible* relationship with doctors and the medical field. This should come as no surprise, as medicine has historically been hostile toward Black people. In the antebellum South, for example, white doctors routinely operated on enslaved Africans without anesthesia. Also, it is believed that modern gynecology was actually developed as a result of dangerous experiments on enslaved Black women by practitioners such as Dr. James Marion Sims. In addition, you may be familiar with the Tuskegee experiment in which doctors knowingly infected Black men with syphilis. There are many stories of medical abuse in the United States. This has caused a traumatic relationship between Black folks and the systems that are ideally supposed to care for them. Black folks approach doctors, and health providers more broadly, with skepticism and well-founded paranoia.

Today, however, this fear creates a medical care aversion that leads to health disparities. Getting the kind of medical care that can help you maintain physical health is a self-care essential. You desperately need a provider for a better quality of life. You need to know the state of your internal body. It's not enough to say that you feel *fine* most days. You deserve better than *fine*. You deserve to feel *good*, maybe even *great*, about your internal health. Imagine the quality of daily life you can have when you are reassured that your health is in check.

The longer you go without seeing a physician, the more you increase the odds that an undiagnosed issue will lead to a critical health outcome. For simple issues, this may not be that big a deal, but I'm sure that you have stories—just as I do—of a friend or relative finally getting to the doctor and receiving devastating news. This is all too common among Black men. By scheduling routine care, you can make sure that you don't become a statistic. You can take control of your health and live a life worth living with the right care. This will enable you to enjoy things in your life and be the man that you need to be for your loved ones.

Take Action

Okay, brother, now is the time. It's okay to feel nervous and very vulnerable when finally taking the step to make that appointment and get that physical. However, you must acknowledge that you can't make the best decisions about your health unless you receive regular medical exams. As a first step, do some research to find a provider that you think could be a good fit for you. And if you're finding it hard to find a suitable provider, ask relatives and friends to make recommendations. Maybe it's something you can do together. Remember, you can exercise self-care by finding a medical home, a place that monitors your health and provides any needed treatment. You've got this!

Rethink Your Relationship with Food

Soul food is almost synonymous with "Black" food, especially in the United States. The relationship between American soul food—items ranging from collard greens to the feet and intestines of pigs—and Black folks is deep. Some historians have described soul food as adapted versions of recipes from our enslaved ancestors. For many of us, this food is not just a cuisine; it is connected to culture and family and represents a shared experience. In the wake of studies on the health impact of some foods, it's important to revisit what we think of as soul nourishing and reexamine the stories we've been told about our food.

Many Black Americans live in food deserts. This means that many Black folks in the United States—especially in inner cities—don't have access to fresh food, fruit, and vegetables. It can be theorized that the complex and often laborious cooking techniques that we have for soul food are, in part, adaptations that mitigated the structures that limited Black access to cooking methods and ingredients. In short, our ancestors had to be very creative with what they had. Because of that creativity, we all get to experience something beautiful, delicious, and meaningful. But that doesn't mean we have to continue consuming soul food at levels we have in the past. People evolve. Cultures evolve, and that's okay.

I love soul food, and you should too! There's no shame in digging into a heaping spoonful of mac and cheese (but only if mama makes it) or sweet potato pie (a personal favorite of mine). Of course, it's important to be mindful of portion size and frequency when it comes to very rich cultural foods. On the other hand, not all soul food is indulgent or overly rich. That's social programming you will need to challenge as well. Everything in moderation, as they say. Enjoy your soul food, but don't make it the primary source of nutrition.

Instead, find ways to increase flavor while cutting back on saturated fats and high-sodium ingredients that contribute to an increased prevalence of hypertension and heart issues in the Black male population. Of course, we can't forget another tension stressor: the lingering impact of intergenerational trauma and racial discrimination. There is no single predictor of health, but by taking action where you can, you can create a better quality of life for a much longer time. And wouldn't it be great to extend your life so that you can spend more time with your partner, family, and other loved ones?

Take Action

Take an honest look at your current diet. Are there places where slight adjustments can make it a bit healthier? Can you cut back on the sodium content? Can you eat more fresh fish and vegetables? Or maybe you can examine how often you are eating very rich soul food? The small adjustments add up, so start by taking this first step today.

Write an Unsent Letter

For us as Black men, it can be difficult to find the right words to communicate our deepest feelings. Historically, Black men have been prevented from developing the language to communicate clearly. How exactly? In addition to the overall racial education gap, many generations of Black men haven't been provided the emotional tools necessary to communicate clearly through the language of feelings (despite a growing desire to do so). Yet you may have found yourself getting feedback from a partner, friend, or family member about how you need to open up. Does that sound familiar?

How do you begin to show up and speak clearly when it always seems like you can't find the right words? How do you strike the balance between being assertive and honest without being aggressive or mean?

One way to do this is to work closely with a therapist to figure out your communication patterns and learn how to communicate clearly in a non-abusive manner. Some of this means unlearning patterns from your own childhood. This is especially true if you were subjected to harsh language from well-intentioned, but also unskilled, communicators for parents.

Another way is to practice! One of the things I've learned as a therapist, is that healthy communication often just takes a bit of practice. In my work with clients, I sometimes use the phrase "emotional rehearsal" to capture the idea of envisioning a conversation or interaction before it happens. You can be actively thinking about the emotions certain messages will convey as you prepare a letter. When you are more prepared, it's easier to find the right words.

You can do this by writing a letter that you do not actually intend to send. This will afford you some time to think critically about what you want to say, review it at your convenience, and revise it before sharing your thoughts with someone.

Take Action

Sit down and write (or type) a draft of a letter for someone involved in your life. It can be a partner, friend, boss, or parent—anyone who is important in your life. In your first draft, write your letter without editing or reviewing it critically. Just go for it, and use any language that makes sense for you. Sleep on it and review it the next day. Does your language sound harsh or unclear? How can you cut down to get to the clearest, simplest expression of your message while still providing necessary detail? For bonus points, have a trusted friend look it over and give you feedback. When you feel you have clarity and your message is concise, practice saying the contents of your unsent letter out loud before sharing your thoughts. You'll get a good feel of how you're sounding and how you may need to adjust to address your concern.

Listen to Your Body

As Black men, we aren't the best at taking time to self-reflect. For many Black men, taking time to check in with yourself feels like a luxury or a privilege reserved for white people or the upper class. It's time to challenge that idea by listening to your body to optimize your health.

Many Black men are stressed by potential threats to personal safety and discrimination in almost every area of life. This is *minority stress,* which, according to Columbia University professor Ilan H. Meyer, is "the excess stress to which individuals from stigmatized social categories are exposed as a result of their social, often a minority, position." The minority stress model refers to this lived reality that any historically oppressed community faces. Research continues to show that stress produces systemic inflammation in the body. This puts the physical health of Black men at particular risk. If you combine the minority stress, Black male hyperfocus on work, and neglect of body signals, this is a recipe for disaster. Eventually, all that stress catches up to you.

Connecting with your body is your first line of defense in taking care of your health. Whether you believe in the merits of therapy and other health practices or not, you must realize that your body is impacted by your environment. If you live in an environment that continually sees your Black body as a threat, then you *feel* that.

All too often, Black people—Black men in particular—are faced with more extreme health issues due to waiting too long to see a health professional. By developing a relationship with your body and learning how it feels to truly be in your skin, you can do a better job of noticing when there is something you need to address.

Take Action

If you're new to intentionally creating a relationship with your body, this might feel uncomfortable at first. Start by sitting back and taking a minute to practice what it feels like to be aware of your body. Do this in a silent room with no distractions as you sit upright. Mentally scan your body and notice what you're sensing. Do you notice tension anywhere? Do your breaths feel deep or shallow? Is there soreness anywhere to speak of? What could help you feel more relaxed in this moment? Perhaps some stretching or mindful breathing would be helpful, or maybe you need to eat and drink some water? Reclaim your body as an important data source for your health right now. Take brief moments like this throughout the day to get the data you need to practice effective self-care.

Take a Mindful Walk

When was the last time you walked purely for pleasure and self-reflection? If you live in a major city, odds are you can find parks and other places to walk. If you live in a more suburban or rural area, you likely have more space. But if you are producing crops or commuting long distances for work or business in a city, you may have fewer opportunities to take mindful walks. However, there are fewer parks and walking paths in or near Black neighborhoods. Black men must find or create paths because walking is not just good exercise. It can also be a powerful tool for your mental health when you apply the principles of mindfulness during strolls.

Mindfulness refers to being present and paying attention to the current moment. This means you do not multitask or allow your focus to wander or be distracted by worries. Mindfulness practitioners often refer to such mental restlessness as "monkey mind." Being mindful has been shown to reduce stress and promote relaxation—and it's safe to say that most people need quite a bit of that in their life.

As a practice, mindfulness is easier said than done and requires practice. Most people, over time, get better at switching from that monkey mind back to more focused thinking during walks. Walking is a relatively automatic process for most people, and it gives you the opportunity for your brain to focus on the experience itself rather than the journey of getting from point A to point B. This is what makes walking a great opportunity to practice mindfulness.

Mindfulness doesn't necessarily require you to act differently; it encourages you to *observe* differently. In this case, it means approaching walking as a means to calm yourself.

Take Action

A mindful walk can be pretty simple. First, you need to identify a safe outdoor path. If you have trouble walking or have mobility issues, you can also do this in a wheelchair or use balance tools such as canes and set your distance within your capacity.

The most important thing about mindful walking is to use the senses available to you to observe your experience. As you walk, pay attention to what you see in the environment around you. Take notice of the landscape or buildings. Try to describe them to yourself by acknowledging all the details. Note the sounds around you. You may hear birds or other animals, car engines, the wind floating around you, or people talking. What do you smell? How does it feel as your feet hit the ground with each step? Does the weather make your skin feel warm or cool? There are no right or wrong answers here. These are opportunities to give yourself permission to fully absorb the moment. Whether you do it for five or fifty minutes is up to you. Make a habit of taking mindful walks to stay present.

Journal on Your Own Terms

Instead of typing or writing out your feelings, you can record a voice memo of your reaction to something or a reflection on your day. The benefits of audio journaling are significant. It's often much more convenient and quicker to share your thoughts and feelings through the spoken word. In addition, if you ever tried journaling when you were younger and had your privacy invaded or the contents of your journal thrown back at you, then you may feel scared to try again. With audio journaling, you can store your thoughts securely via password protection. Another benefit of audio journaling is that you only need one device to do it (and your phone is the one thing you likely *always* have on you). Also, when you revisit your audio notes, you can detect the mood and tone of your voice, which offers a different level of insight than just the written words used in traditional journaling.

Self-reflection via audio also gives you the opportunity to speak in the way that feels most comfortable and natural for you. Many of us have negative experiences with writing throughout school, and Black people especially face harsh criticism for using AAVE (African-American Vernacular English). Journaling is meant to be your private space for reflection. You don't need to code-switch here or focus on trying to be someone who journals "the right way."

The most important thing with self-reflection is that you do it in a way that feels authentic and comfortable for you. Nothing else matters here.

Take Action

Take out your phone right now and record a voice memo to this prompt: "What's one thing from your day that you wished would've worked out differently, and why? How did you feel about it?" Use the language and words that feel most natural, and honest, to you. Don't worry about anyone else needing to understand what you mean. This is your space to speak freely, without judgment, and on your own terms. You can choose to share some pieces of this recording with other people later if it makes sense to, but that's not the point of audio journaling. The point is to give yourself permission to express how you feel without worrying about how you'll be perceived. You deserve that space.

Try Floating

Odds are you have never heard of floating before, and that's okay. Floating is a self-care practice that takes place in a sensory deprivation space. This is a fancy way of saying that you are in a pod or tank of some sort, alone and in the dark, in a pool of water infused with Epsom salt (magnesium sulfate), so you float easily above water level.

One of the great things about this world is that there are so many ways to practice self-care and wellness. Yet much of the information out there isn't marketed toward Black men. That doesn't mean, however, that it can't be a good thing for you or isn't worth trying.

Floating involves stepping into a pod filled with highly salted water (like the Dead Sea). You lie back and float in the water with limited noise and distraction. I first came across floating many years ago when I was feeling a lot of stress and pressure. At that time, floating was still relatively new in the mainstream, and it was becoming a topic of conversation in the wellness space as a strategy to promote relaxation. The low-stimulation environment helps put your nervous system at rest, and the salt and magnesium help relieve body tension.

This is not for everyone, particularly if you are claustrophobic, have a fear of darkness, or have a water phobia. While it is extremely safe, floating can be challenging for many people.

If you are ready to explore this, try searching for "float tank," "sensory deprivation," or "float therapy" near you. Most often, you'll find float therapy centers in and around major cities. There is a lot of variation here, as some floating spots give you the option for lights or music to help you keep your composure. Others require you to do the full sensory deprivation experience in complete darkness and silence for the duration of your float.

In this pod, you lie in a pool of water that is saturated with Epsom salt, which provides buoyancy as well as calming elements that help reduce blood pressure. What's special about this experience is that floating gives you the illusion of weightlessness. You can do it for as few as fifteen minutes to up to an hour in many places.

Here's why floating could be helpful for you. How often do you feel that you have *the weight of the world* on your shoulders? How much do you find yourself struggling to make ends meet or provide for your family? How often do you get to feel free from those responsibilities? Most Black men never get that kind of break. Floating might be a good way to quiet your mind and experience weightlessness. In addition, floating gives you a new way of experiencing your body and can be great to try when you've been feeling stuck in your life generally. New experiences can often help provide clarity and aid in discovering what needs to happen on the journey moving forward.

Take Action

If floating sounds like something you would be interested in, head to the Internet and do a bit more research on it. Search for floating centers in and around your city if you'd like to try it. Those with health issues such as low blood pressure and claustrophobia probably should not float. As with any health or wellness practice, it's good to consult with your doctor first if you have any concerns. Give yourself permission to experience a sense of weightlessness.

Allow Yourself to Feel

One of the things I've discovered about many Black men is that it's difficult for them to softly embrace their feelings.

You might even be cringing right now. That's okay. But hear me out.

Most Black men have embraced the dominant culture's definition of what it means to be a man. Most often, that means having a cool and very relaxed posture—as if you are never bothered much by anything. For the prize of displaying the masculine ideal, you completely suppress many feelings. For example, the refusal to acknowledge anything that makes you feel vulnerable and weak is a manifestation of this suppression. It's time to free yourself from these constraints. Black men can improve their relationships and their mental health by connecting with their emotions.

Feelings provide you with data about your internal experience with something, which is helpful information. Allowing yourself to feel requires you to do some decoding. For example, when you experience the emotion of guilt, it may be because you think you've done something wrong. And, let's face it, it can be hard as a man to admit when you've made a mistake. Acknowledging those feelings can also make you feel inadequate and weak. You might deny your feelings and pretend to be unbothered to compensate for these softer feelings. Everyone does this from time to time. The hope is that denial is not the primary way in which you respond to your feelings. If so, you're likely not maturing emotionally, and your relationships and mental health will suffer as a result.

But here's what I need you to understand, dear brother: Softness is your birthright. It may sound strange to read, but every person on this planet may access and hold those tender feelings. This is part of the human experience. It doesn't make you less of a man to acknowledge a moment in which you don't feel worthy or adequate. It doesn't make you any less of a man to acknowledge that feeling vulnerable makes you feel small and ashamed. You can work through those feelings, but not if you always ignore them and lock them inside yourself. Give yourself grace in knowing that you can be a man and acknowledge a feeling that doesn't make you feel strong.

Take Action

Take a moment right now to reflect on an emotional experience, a memory you've been trying to suppress. Perhaps you made a mistake at work, an error that caused you to feel inadequate or defensive. Perhaps your partner did something that made you feel insecure or worried. You can work toward speaking your truth moving forward, but for right now, just try to take a moment to give yourself the space to identify what you're feeling. Affirm that it is okay that you're having these feelings and acknowledge that you don't know what to do with them just yet. Remind yourself that feelings have no gender and that you don't have to respond to your feelings with male-centered judgment and self-criticism that stems from dominant-culture thinking.

Try a New Spiritual Practice

While there are some Black men involved in religious or spiritual circles, a disproportionate number are ministers, lay assistants such as deacons, and aspirant followers of church leaders. A larger number of Black men don't participate in church, and many believe that spirituality or religious services oare women's domain. Churches are fulfilling for many. However, you don't have to attend church services to find or create meditative spiritual practices that enable you to relate more empathetically to people and your environment in a loving and aware manner.

Let me begin by saying that every person has the right to identify with any religion or spiritual practice. That applies to the agnostics and atheists willing to explore new kinds of body-mind connections. The goal here is to provide you with the opportunity to look at the role of spirituality in your life more broadly. If this is *not* something that interests you at all, it's perfectly valid to ignore this entry and move on. However, if there's some part of you that's curious about this area of your life, take a moment to sit with this idea of trying something new.

Many men are rooted in very practical things. For a lot of Black men, this can make the world of spirituality feel illusive or untouchable. To illustrate this point, take a moment to reflect on how it feels when you're at or leaving a religious service. Do you feel a deep personal connection to the experience and what it means for your life? Or do you often feel that it's more like a spiritual paint-by-numbers exercise during which you're just doing what you're supposed to do and hoping for the best? While many men are devout in some form of faith, many don't allow themselves to experience something that feels more abstract—something that moves beyond a specific doctrine and creates an internal experience that better connects them to the world around them.

Take Action

This is an opportunity to push yourself outside of your comfort zone and try something new spiritually. This may be reconnecting with prayer. It may also involve visiting a spot in nature and thinking about how to contribute to the environment around you. Or visiting a different kind of religious service to find new inspirations, or finding awareness and quiet joy by spending time in reflection by the ocean. Whatever form it takes, explore your spirituality. Consider how you can continue to develop and heal in this aspect of your life moving forward.

Stop Responding When Someone Calls You "Bro" (Unless You're Okay with That)

Black men are some of the smoothest men on the planet. We can own that and feel pride about that. But, as a result, many people get entirely too comfortable with any Black man they come across. They quickly adopt a language that they assume will be comfortable for all Black men. As a person, you're entitled to have your own standards. You can set limits on how you want people to refer to you by how you respond—or by not responding at all.

You don't always have to answer when someone wants to call you something other than your name. This runs counter to a lot of indoctrinated messaging Black men have received—the notion that "you've got to go along to get along." This is still true in many respects, but it's also important to challenge the notion that you always have to shrink for the benefit of other people's comfort and ease. You know there are always considerations you need to take when setting boundaries with others because—as you do—you risk being perceived as overly aggressive. This is a burden that Black men bear, and it is exhausting! It's okay to lay that burden down on some occasions.

This isn't to say that no one can ever call you "Bro," "Bruh," or anything else. But you also don't have to accept dictates on how you should be addressed. You can determine how you want to be addressed and how you want to manage that.

You get to set limits with the people around you, no matter the environment. For far too long, Black men have been expected to succumb to norms that don't apply to others. That can range from accepting or rejecting the language people use around us to broader systemic forces that dictate how we're supposed to live our lives. But times are changing, and you are no longer required to tolerate someone referring to you in a manner that makes you uncomfortable. You get to correct and redirect someone who refers to you by the wrong name or talks to you in a way that suggests they're overly familiar. This is about personal dignity. Dignity gives you the power to say "no" or ignore someone who refuses to acknowledge you in the way you have requested.

Take Action

Take a moment to consider the words people often use to refer to you that are not your name. Are you comfortable with how people are engaging you? If not, what should that be changed to? Take some time to reflect on this, and brainstorm how you might assertively address the issue head-on the next time it happens in an interaction.

Challenge Impostor Syndrome

You may have heard the term "impostor syndrome" floating around a lot more these days. It refers to *internalized* feelings of fear, self-doubt, worries, and inferiority that lead to increased stress and performance issues when you reach a higher level in your career. You might have experienced these feelings as you have tried to climb the company ladder. However, that doesn't mean you suffer from this "syndrome." Those claiming Black men disproportionately suffer from the syndrome ignore the role of race-based roadblocks in the workplace as the source of stress.

The claim that Black men are suffering from this syndrome is often leveled by a company's white managers, who are extensions of the powers that be. In fact, in many cases, the people in charge have created work environments that make Black men feel insecure and inferior. To put it plainly, corporatism and capitalism have pathologized employees' reactions to the prejudicial and often racist components of their system. In other words, they've turned the reality of institutional bias into an employee competency issue, particularly as it relates to assessments of Black men.

Black men, other People of Color, women of all races and ethnicities, and Queer folks have systematically been kept out of the upper echelon of the corporate structure throughout history. Bias in corporate recruitment and subjective employee evaluation practices have prompted marginalized people to understate their value and, in some cases, question their competency. This works, most often, to benefit the white, upper-class, heterosexual men who own and wrote the societal playbook. This means that if you don't "act right" in those spaces, you will not progress in your career. And they will tell you it's because you just don't feel like "corporate material."

Feeling like an impostor in places that aren't supportive of your success is not a personal failure. It is a reasonable reaction to intentional exclusionary practices. You may have work you need to do to be successful in these environments. Many stay in these environments because there are no other comparable job opportunities. After all, you have to provide for yourself and your family. Understandably, you do everything you can (e.g., code-switching) to be successful. You also deserve to not feel unworthy and stress yourself out internally when you realize the problems are external.

Take Action

The next time you find yourself feeling like an impostor with a new challenge or role in your career, take a moment to make an honest assessment of your skills and work history. What have you done well? What would your employer referrals say about your capacity to perform and produce work? Then say to yourself, "This anxiety is not of my own creation," and place the onus where it belongs—on a system that still works to make it harder for you to achieve. Offer yourself compassion, and keep doing what you need to do to get where you want to go. You are deserving and unstoppable.

Debrief from Vicarious Trauma

After Ahmaud Arbery was murdered in 2020, the simple anticipation of lacing up my shoes and leaving my house put me on the floor in tears. All too often we see the lives of Black men, who look like us and our family members, dying at the hands of police or bigoted vigilantes. How are you supposed to feel okay going out in the world when scrolling online leads you to yet another unjust killing—a new name and another hashtag? It's important to acknowledge the negative impact this has on your mental health. You can take care of your mental health by creating space to understand and debrief after these kinds of events.

Sometimes it feels like second nature to just go numb and live in denial. It's painful and terrifying to realize that some people are willing to attack you because they fear and/or hate you. They often feel that way because you are different in appearance—you are *the other*. This is the burden of racism that has existed for centuries. The impact of this thinking throughout history has generated atrocities such as the transatlantic slave trade, the Holocaust, and Jim Crow terror in the American South.

Some like to believe this extreme thinking is buried in the past. Yet, these days, you are faced with examples of racist violence in the modern day. Your morning news show covers the story. Friends talk about it online. A coworker may even want to check in about it at work. These losses are all around you, but how often do you take a moment to honestly reflect on the toll it takes on your heart and spirit? You are stressed, but you try to move on without processing each event, maybe because you believe there isn't enough time or energy to or you don't consider it a priority.

Well, you must begin to make time to debrief. You can respond to such events by finding spaces online or in the community to discuss your thoughts and feelings to reduce stress and build a social support network that will enable you to keep moving forward in your life.

Take Action

Identify a couple of places you could visit when you need more support and time to debrief. It could be, for example, a barbershop, house of worship, or community center. It's also good to have a few individuals you can rely on for debriefings as well. This could come in the form of a friend, a support group for men, or a therapist. Try to put these resources in place before the next time you need them. Do not minimize your feelings and work through this all alone.

Learn Your Toxic Traits

There is a lot of discussion about men and Black masculinity these days. Definitions of masculinity are changing rapidly. That often prompts Black men to try to determine the corrosive factors that make relationships with other people more difficult. Every person on this earth can act in toxic ways. No one is exempt. And, for most of us, this toxicity is realized in everyday interactions. Being a responsible, accountable man also means giving yourself room to explore how you may have been toxic and then become better for the future.

Black men are no exception to this kind of self-examination. As hard as it can be to hear, meaningful self-exploration and adjustment are necessary for sustainable, healthy relationships. Some examples of toxic behavior may have shown up in your life in the following ways: thinking that you are right in every situation, shutting down when you want to avoid an emotional conversation, and dictating what others say or can do. Human beings are social creatures, and we all need to be mindful of our behavior if we want satisfying relationships and opportunities to help define a masculinity that is more society friendly. That means doing the work to identify how your actions might be considered problematic or toxic. Toxicity can show up in your life in many ways, but it's important to remember that just because you do something toxic doesn't make you unworthy or a toxic person. It means that you have some work to do—as we all do.

When faced with criticism about something you've frequently done or said, it's hard not to take it personally and become defensive. This is your psyche defending itself because that feedback doesn't match up to the picture you have of yourself. This is a normal human reaction.

The reality is that we are not the best judges of our own character. We must move beyond that knee-jerk defensiveness to seriously consider the feedback we get from others. Sometimes, while your intentions are not malicious, it is entirely possible to hurt those around you. Your intent doesn't absolve you from being held accountable for your actions.

Take Action

Create some time and space for quiet reflection. In this space, try to reflect on the feedback you've received from people in your life until this point. What are the common threads or themes in their feedback? Have you gotten feedback that you shut down in more emotional conversations and stop talking? Have you been told you respond with rage to even minor inconveniences? Are you comfortable being seen this way? If these traits tend to get in the way of your relationships—romantic, platonic, familial, professional—consider how you could adjust moving forward and what supports you will need to make those adjustments happen. Some men actually experience emotional overwhelm during highly emotional conversations, and this leads to shutting down, almost automatically. Adjustment may look like finding ways to calm yourself in the moment or briefly pausing so that you can stay invested in the conversation at hand.

Adjust Your Relationship with Anger and Rage

Anger is a normal human emotion. For some people, anger is an emotion that's hard to access and express, but for many Black men, anger and irritability are often very accessible. When I think about anger—especially as it relates to Black men—I'm reminded of the quote from the acclaimed author and activist James Baldwin. He said: "To be a Negro in this country and to be relatively conscious is to be in a state of rage almost all of the time." Black men must understand this rage and make necessary adjustments.

Anger gets a bad rap, but it is a useful emotion. As it relates to Black men, anger is often one of the primary defenses. It helps us respond to upsetting social situations. Research in 2006 from psychologists Jennifer Lerner and Larissa Tiedens in the *Journal of Behavioral Decision Making* shows that in the aftermath of anger, there can be increases in optimism and performance. Also, a 2004 study published in the *Journal of Personality and Social Psychology* suggests that expressing anger can lead to more successful negotiations in life or on the job. Anger on its own is not good or bad—it's what you do with it that matters.

To be sure, anger helps Black men manage the enduring pain of consistently being denied full humanity in the eyes of society. But you are more than your rage. It cannot consume you.

This caution is necessary because many Black men—out of habit derived from frequent past transgressions—become angry in situations that don't require that emotion. This can create divides between you and your associates and loved ones. This means you can miss out on true feelings of kindness from an associate or a friend. Anger can also destroy intimacy between you and a loved one. Consider this: If you're always so well prepared with anger to defend yourself, it becomes harder and harder to express the respect and affection you have for people in your life.

You may not have permitted yourself to let some of that anger go because you're afraid you will be hurt as a result. However, the risk is worth it. You deserve to experience the fullness of life without anger in the driver's seat. Peace and deep healing wait for you on the other side.

Take Action

The next time you feel yourself reacting immediately out of anger or frustration, take a deep breath and imagine that beyond that anger might be another emotion that needs your attention. Could hurt or fear be underneath that anger? If so, moving forward may look like identifying the added support you need to feel more at peace, which may look like debriefing with a loved one or trusted professional. Moving forward may also look like exploring ways to feel safer in your space or seeking reassurance in a relationship. Using this technique, you can learn how to respond to anger without letting it be your unconscious driver.

Lean Into Vulnerability

These days, men are asked to reevaluate the relationship between masculinity and vulnerability. For many men, especially Black men, the integration of the two has not historically been a highly held value. That's not an indictment but more of the recognition that the Black man's relationship with vulnerability is largely tied to the intergenerational trauma of enslaved ancestors being beaten and abused. At that time, a display of vulnerability was seen as a weakness that would likely lead to death. Avoiding vulnerability and projecting strength are thus part of your survival response. But you don't need to have the same kind of armor today. You can benefit by leaning into your vulnerabilities.

You may have grown up in a home that readily saw vulnerability as something only for women and weak men. To be vulnerable meant opening yourself to pain and even violence. If "soft" has ever been hurled at you—or you've said it to another man—you likely know how effective it can be in controlling someone and hardening him. Maybe you've experienced being shamed or made fun of because you dared to share something that was bothering you. All too often, little Black boys have these experiences in their homes, schools, and social environments. This gives you the early message that showing up in the world in a way that looks too "sensitive" is okay for other people, but not for you. Even the most well-intentioned parents parrot this message to keep their little Black boys safe in a world hell-bent on silencing them. This is survival. If you are still not allowing yourself to truly be vulnerable with the people around you, you are still only surviving.

It's time to thrive.

Thriving means leaning into your vulnerability. It means you allow for the possibility that your soft spots—or the tender parts of you—will be exposed. This may put you at a higher risk of being shamed, judged, or worse. But it also means that those parts might get support. Therein lies the calculated risk of vulnerability.

You will need to share that small moment when your partner made an off-the-cuff comment that rubbed you the wrong way. You will need to ask a friend to help when you're struggling with a personal problem. You will need to find a person, or counselor, to create a safe space for you to process the anxieties, fears, and anger that come with being a Black man living in today's world. As you do that, you'll thrive and your mental health will improve. Anger will feel more manageable. You will understand what it means to *feel* love and give it right back.

Take Action

Start now by practicing a bit of vulnerability with yourself. Take a moment to tap into the last few days or weeks and reflect on what's been on your mind. What is coming up for you? What hurt, pain, or frustration rises to the surface? Take a moment just to sit with that feeling and allow it to wash over you without judgment. You have a right to feel whatever you feel without justification. This is your space to be vulnerable.

When you're ready, text a friend or reach out to a loved one and simply ask them to listen. Try your best to not doubt yourself or get caught up in how they might view what you say. Stay focused on sharing what you can to experience the relief of finally getting something off your chest.

Take an Honest Look at Your Mental Health

In the past few years, we have made great strides in embracing mental health in the Black community. The growing interest among Black men has been boosted partly because high-profile rappers such as Lil Wayne and Kid Cudi have publicly discussed their mental health challenges. More and more Black men now realize that many of us have mental health challenges, and we need to acknowledge them honestly as the initial self-care step to managing them.

Historically, people with mental health issues have been stigmatized in the Black community. The reasons for this are complicated on both societal and individual levels. For those with treatment needs, there have been concerns about stigmatization and a very real fear of what would happen if they went to the exam room of a mental health facility. This stems from an awareness of medical experimentation on African Americans—among them, the infamous Tuskegee experiment, a federal health project. From 1932 to 1972, federal officials inflicted many unknowing Black men with syphilis and left them untreated to study the long-term effects.

Considering such events, you can easily understand why the National Alliance on Mental Illness has stated that only 30 percent of Black men get the mental healthcare they need in the United States each year. Also, when you're not exposed to information on mental health, it is hard to determine whether you need treatment. Fortunately, more Black men are now willing to learn about mental health and what untreated mental illness looks like in real life.

After learning these facts, Black men can then make an honest self-assessment of their condition. A good place to start is to take an inventory of how you've been feeling. For many Black men, even taking a few minutes to do this feels unnecessary or like a luxury. Or you may feel uncomfortable recalling incidents and/or thoughts that raise red flags about your condition. It may not feel easy, but it's an important step.

This is important because mental health impacts everything in your life. Treatment can help you understand how you feel, and why, about the world around you, your relationships, and your workplace. This is not a luxury; it's a necessity. It is also urgent because the mental state of Black men can be affected by discrimination, overt racism, and the ongoing spate of racially motivated deadly physical attacks.

Take Action

There are helpful resources out there that enable you to receive objective assessments of your mental health. For example, mental health professionals use screening tools, such as the GAD-7 for anxiety, PHQ-9 for depression, and PCL-5 for post-traumatic stress disorder. These practitioners diagnose before they treat. Practitioners can also train you to self-monitor your condition between health appointments. However, this process cannot begin until you're honest with yourself about your mental health and the need for professional support.

Rethink the Strong Black Man Trope

Liberation is about freeing yourself to create a life of outcomes that *you* want. To do that, you will need to resist the trope of always being the strong Black man.

There is nothing wrong with wanting to be a strong Black man. It's not necessarily problematic. Yet there is also an unwavering belief that Black men are the prototypes of strength and stability. Why do many people believe that? And more importantly, what does that belief cost you?

Let's start with why. The truth is that none of us would be here without the strength and mental fortitude of our ancestors. Yet we often forget that much more than the stereotypical idea of "strength" got us to where we are today. Black men have had to be strong to survive in the world. You may live in a neighborhood that requires you to project a particular kind of strength or masculinity so that you don't become someone's next victim. You need another strength—mental fortitude—to walk into a boardroom as the only Black man present. However, there is so much more to Black men's strength than these examples.

Most men are taught that to be strong means to be unwavering and absolute. If you try to live up to that definition, it can create tightly wound tension that releases itself by being stereotypically strong instead of wise. Yes, good judgment can also be a strength. You also need resiliency—another strength—and the power of empathy to relate to people in difficult situations. It also takes strength to ask for help because no one can do it all alone—not even the strongest Black man. You need to recognize that no man can do everything perfectly all the time. You need space to mess up and fall apart too. And once you do, you have to be strong enough to put yourself back together again.

A single-minded definition of strength goes against what is known about survival and growth. No being can move forward without the help of others. No being can dole out strength and protection 100 percent of the time. The best example of this is Mother Nature herself. There is a natural rhythm, an ebb and flow, of strength and weakness—of damage and recovery. This is how the world continues to spin despite the harm being done to it daily. When was the last time you acknowledged the hurt you were carrying? Also, when was the last time you made time and space to recover?

Take Action

It can be hard to redefine what strength looks like when it has been framed in one particular way your entire life. At this moment, try to come up with five words or phrases that reflect the kind of strength you'd like to gain and use in the future. Strength can mean being brave enough to face your feelings honestly and share them with others. It can also mean the courage to seek help and support when life feels too hard to deal with on your own. On the other hand, you can also rethink any Superman-like notions and free yourself of the feeling that you always have to show up in the world as "strong." Repeat "I don't have to be strong right now" or "My feelings deserve care and attention too" as much and as often as you need to.

Give Yourself Space to Cry

Crying is often seen as a sign of weakness, as well as woman-like, but that could not be further from the truth. In my experience as a therapist, crying can give you a cathartic release. Black men don't access this enough.

While you may not necessarily see crying as weak, think about the number of times you've seen another Black man cry. More than likely, that number is tiny—and there's a reason for that. You can recognize that cultural standards make crying a difficult emotional response for most Black men. It's not seen as a valid reaction to anything that's emotionally heavy. However, you also recognize that some things do rattle you or cause you pain, right? That begs the question: Where does all the pent-up energy and feeling go?

You can free yourself from this emotional straitjacket by allowing yourself to express your sorrow or unhappiness. If you can start to allow yourself the mental room to cry, you can express *and release* what's inside. Without this kind of release, internal tension increases. This produces stress and contributes to declining physical health. And for Black people, chronic stress has been linked to high blood pressure and heart problems.

It might be hard to imagine that crying is okay for anything other than a funeral for a lot of men. There are also plenty of us so disconnected from how we feel in those heavier moments that—even then—tears don't fall from our eyes. Self-care requires you to allow yourself a fuller range of emotions.

Take Action

Not many people can cry on cue, and that's not the point here. Giving yourself space to cry means first reducing the barriers that leave you shut off from the more vulnerable parts of yourself. Take a few moments to reflect on what barriers stand in the way of you being more vulnerable with yourself. Is it cultural conditioning? Is it difficult circumstances from your family history? Or some mixture of the two? Take one step today to address one of those barriers. For example, you may consider talking to a friend about your struggles with this. Or you could seek professional support from a therapist. Or you could track your emotions by making periodic entries in a journal. Take this step.

Practice Gratitude with the G.L.A.D. Technique

Considering that organizations and institutions involved in wellness are largely white and very female, there should be no surprise that very few Black men participate in their health programs. Unfortunately, this means we Black men often miss out on very practical techniques to better our mental health, like the G.L.A.D. strategy. This daily practice can help you acknowledge the positivity in your life, providing a much-needed buffer to the real-world stressors around you.

The G.L.A.D. acronym stands for G(ratitude), L(earned), A(chieved), and D(elight). It's the simple practice of writing down things you feel grateful (G) for, and/or one thing you have learned (L), and/or something you've achieved or accomplished (A), and one thing you've just found delightful (D). That's it! You write one thing for each of those letters, no matter how big or small, important or not.

The idea is to make this a regular practice (possibly daily) to get the best results. As you practice gratitude regularly, the theory is that you will begin to notice more positive things more often. Essentially, you're training yourself to see more positives by practicing seeing the positives consistently. This helps adjust your perspective and improve your mood in just a few minutes per day.

Gratitude has become a popular tool in mental health self-care due to the positive psychology movement of the 1980s. Instead of focusing on mental health from a pathological perspective, such as focusing on what's "wrong" with you, positive psychology seeks to explore what practices and things we need to generate happiness. This kind of positive psychology can appear disconnected from people's real lives, especially when it's presented with glossy magazine-type images by white influencers. It can look like not living in the real world. But that doesn't mean that there isn't something positive to take away. We just have to dig a bit deeper to see if, and how, it can apply to us.

Gratitude, as a practice, is likely one of those things you've come across online. With roots in eastern traditions such as Buddhism, a gratitude practice involves consciously making note of things that are good and positive in your life. This can be hard to do if you don't think there's much positive in your life at the moment.

This can be of great value to Black men because there are so many negative experiences, it can be difficult to acknowledge the good things happening in your life. But there are always good things, no matter how small, to pay attention to. For some people, the idea of simply saying what you're grateful for feels too flat or disingenuous when other things are going on. I appreciate the G.L.A.D. technique because it involves more than saying, "I'm grateful for X."

Take Action

Now, it's your turn. In the next few minutes, write down something from your day that you felt grateful for, something you learned, something you completed or achieved, and something that just made you smile. Practice G.L.A.D. daily and consistently for the best results.

Take a Depression Screener

If you were to look at mental health statistics for Black men, you would notice that the rate of depression among Black men is low at around 5–10 percent as of 2023, even when compared to Black women (around 14 percent). Do you think Black men are less susceptible to depression than Black women and other groups?

While that might be nice to believe, it's probably not true. Statistics themselves are facts, but it always makes sense to take time to think about them critically. Researchers have suggested that part of the reason why the rates of depression among Black men are so low is that there simply aren't enough men coming forward and talking about their mental health. That's one reason Black men who believe they are depressed should get medical screening to determine whether they have the condition.

Depression disrupts the brain's ability to think rationally. It can easily make you think that there is something deeply wrong with you—as in, "I'm just not a good person." Over-personalizing emotional pain is a significant threat to Black men's mental health. It reinforces self-critical thinking and keeps you from getting the help you need. If you have been struggling recently, have you considered that depression isn't a moral failing but a response to ongoing societal pressure, trauma, and discrimination?

There is a common misconception that for someone to be depressed, they must feel sad or down. This is certainly true for many people who deal with depression, but not for everyone, especially Black men. Depression tends to look different on Black folks. Instead of appearing sad, a depressed Black man may be more likely to experience ongoing anger and irritability. He may also get through his days by not feeling very much at all (numbness). "I'm cool" is one of the most socially acceptable ways for Black men to cover up feeling numb and disconnected. If this sounds like you, then it might be worth exploring if you may be dealing with depression.

Depression is not a one-size-fits-all condition but more so a cluster of symptoms of different depressive conditions that can look and sound alike. Taking an assessment can help provide insight and clarity.

Take Action

Schedule an appointment with a primary care doctor to get a mental health referral or arrange to see a licensed therapist to determine whether you are suffering from a form of depression. Practitioners will conduct a brief assessment, such as the PHQ-9, to help you find answers to what you've been experiencing. You can review a depression assessment online before taking this step. However, you should always try to verify information you've received online by obtaining confirmation and treatment recommendations from licensed providers.

Reexamine Your Relationship with Your Body

We Black men have a complicated relationship with our bodies. On one hand, we are taught to believe that our bodies are pillars of superior strength and sexual energy. On the other hand, as bodies inevitably change or health issues arise, it can be difficult to look at yourself with the same kind of pride and admiration.

Part of the problem is our overidentification with the body. This stems from the slave trade. As enslaved Africans were kidnapped and sold, they lost the right to do what they pleased with their bodies. During slavery, Black men were referenced based on how big or small they were and how many hours they could labor in a day before collapsing. Black folks were made to ignore their body's cues of exhaustion and the need for more sustenance and better working conditions. In some ways, the Black body became a production unit. It was a means for white slavers to enrich themselves. Stories told by slave owners focused on the "brute" strength and "savage" sexual nature of Black men because their so-called owners also wanted more future slaves.

Unfortunately, this is one way in which slavery continues to negatively impact the psyche of the Black man today. Many of us have unconsciously internalized these kinds of values.

There's nothing wrong with having pride in physical strength, endurance, and sexual ability. However, adopting a healthier relationship with your body requires looking at it more comprehensively. Instead of reducing the value of your body to your capacity to move heavy objects or sexually satisfy a partner, consider the other things that your body does and how it enriches your life and the lives of those around you.

What does that mean exactly? It means that your body is the vessel that carries you throughout your daily life. It's more than what makes you valuable in the eyes of greater society and capitalism. Your body enables you to support yourself and your family. On a personal level, it enables you to do or experience things you enjoy—from listening to music to creating art to exploring the beauty of nature around you.

Take Action

Take a moment to recognize your body for something that it provides, or allows you to do, outside of the realm of sexual performance, strength, and productivity. Does it give you the energy to provide for your family? Does your body allow you to create works of art? Does it allow you to hold your daughter's hands as she takes her first steps? From here on out, make it a daily practice to value your body for something it does to help the people most important in your life. Reconnect with its purpose beyond sex, strength, and productivity.

Acknowledge an Act of Resistance

Just as it is important to develop new ways of countering racism and discrimination, it is also important to celebrate the moments that you challenged oppression.

One of the vestiges of colonization and the enslavement of African peoples is an internalization of the idea that we must "go along to get along." This perspective is promoted by moderate white politicians who attempt to engender equality by trying to make Black folks appear more palatable and safer to white people in power. Black people do not have this same luxury of waiting until they are deemed "safe."

I've yet to come across a Black person who has not challenged the stories and stereotypes placed upon them. Most Black men feel better about themselves when they have found ways to push back against oppression. As the world continues to reveal itself in all its gloriously racist ways, it can seem that you're not able to do much to advance the state of Black men in this world. And, if you have any doubt about the challenges faced by Black men, it's easy enough to turn on the news and see the ongoing manifestations of bias and prejudice.

But your efforts are not in vain! While every Black person must do what is necessary to thrive in systems built upon routine subjugation and dehumanization, you must not lose hope in your ability to challenge these systems. That hope is the change that the world needs. Reject the thought that you can do or have done nothing. Challenging a racist comment by a coworker or raising questions about the fairness of your company's hiring and promotion practices is a very real act of resistance. While it is important to do as much as you reasonably can to better the standing of your community, no one person does it alone. As a hardworking person in this world, sometimes you need (and deserve!) to pat yourself on the back. Resisting is never easy.

Take Action

This is your chance to gas yourself up a bit. It might feel disingenuous at first, but keep in mind that so many of the ways that you respond to the world around you have become second nature by necessity. After all, no one can do "the work" twenty-four hours a day, seven days a week. However, if you prompt change, even though that was not your conscious objective, you should still pat yourself on the back. Additionally, it is critical to not internalize hopelessness. At times, resisting can seem futile as you face the complexity and enormity of the effort required to create change.

Acknowledging your impact and your small acts of resistance honors the energy and fight you have within you. Reflect now on when you were challenged by bias or overt racism. Pause for a beat and acknowledge your contribution. After that, continue fighting the good fight.

Build Community with Your LGBTQIA+ Family

During the early days of my training in counseling psychology, it was commonplace for teachers and professors to reflect on how Black communities were much more biased against LGBTQIA+ people. Not only is this factually questionable, but it also becomes a self-fulfilling prophecy when we act biased even though we are not.

Increasing critical consciousness is one of the deep values of liberation psychology. This means challenging your cultural programming. Reexamination is a stop on the path toward both internal and communal healing. One idea that must be challenged is the false notion that homosexuality and Queer identities more broadly are somehow products of white colonization. This is not true.

Queer history tells us that Queer folks have existed in all communities and all recorded historical periods. Sure, members of LGBTQIA+ communities may now speak differently because they have left the shadows, but these sexualities are in no way new, and they're not a result of colonization. For example, in Africa, and around the world, female husbands have long existed, as well as same-gender-loving people—a term most frequently used by those in the African Diaspora instead of "gay." Lesbians, transgender people, and other gender non-conforming people have existed for centuries. The knowledge is there if you are open to seeking it.

Raising consciousness means taking time to consider your feelings outside of doctrine and dogma. You can help expand the community of people seeking justice by recognizing and working with LGBTQIA+ people, especially those in your own racial/ethnic community.

Loving Black people and loving Blackness means loving Black LGBTQIA+ people. For many Black Queer folks living at that intersection of identities, the love for Blackness is often unrequited because of the ignorance of many straight Black people. Black Queer folks such as Bayard Rustin and Alicia Garza have been at the forefront of Black liberation movements. The Black Lives Matter movement has Black Queer women among its leaders. Black Queer folks have made all of our lives better and continue doing the work of advancing social justice and equity for all.

Take Action

Try to find a way to build relations with LGBTQIA+ Black folks. If you are Black and LGBTQIA+, you've likely already made your connections in the community. Use those connections to get more Queer involvement in social justice campaigns for all people. If you are a straight Black man, this is your call to action to cultivate community with your LGBTQIA+ brothers and sisters. If this is new for you, it may be intimidating to think about approaching Queer spaces. That's okay. You can start by visiting a local LGBTQIA+ center to find new comrades. Celebrating Blackness means doing so in all its forms and creating safety for every Black person. Here's your opportunity to do so for Black LGBTQIA+ folks if you haven't already. Community care is self-care.

Communicate Assertively

One of the most difficult things about being a man these days is not knowing how to communicate properly. One of the frequent challenges involving couples and families is that men are being asked to step up to the plate and speak openly about their issues. This can be especially difficult for Black men when they haven't been given the skills to communicate effectively.

The fact that so many Black families struggle with open and transparent communication suggests that it is also one of the vestiges of chattel slavery. For the ancestors of Black enslaved people, communication has always been a difficult task. This was, in part, by design. One of the top priorities of slaveholders in the US was to limit communications of the enslaved. The oppressors recognized that language was powerful. They realized that language would help people to organize, rebel, and possibly liberate themselves. The beauty is that Black folks still found incredibly intelligent ways to communicate, often hiding coded messages in songs and stories.

These days, we have a lot more skills and a lot more knowledge about how to communicate and galvanize as a community. We've seen that play out in the Black Lives Matter movement and other social justice movements. However, strain still exists within interpersonal communication between partners and family members. This ability to express ourselves clearly without aggressive, violent language is still a struggle for many Black men. Maybe you've gotten feedback from people in your own life. The good news is there is a clear path forward.

One of the most helpful ways to communicate assertively is by using what I call the XYZ method. The format is "I felt X when you did Y, and I would like Z." This method doesn't necessarily provide a structure for every type of assertive communication, but it provides a good foundation for communicating in a way that is clear about your needs in a non-aggressive way. It also does the work of centering your thoughts or feelings rather than finger-pointing, which is a common pitfall of healthy communication. "I" statements are *very* important in relationships. They help reduce defensiveness and lead to more productive conversations. This approach also helps reinforce the kind of patience, compassion, and authenticity that most partners seek in intimate relationships.

Take Action

Now that you have this format for communicating assertively, take a few moments with yourself to think about a recent situation in which you held back or didn't communicate exactly what you were thinking or feeling for whatever reason. Maybe you held back too much, or you overdid it and came off too harsh. Write out that previous concern using this XYZ method. When you feel ready, try to put this into practice and speak to the person who did something that upset you or wronged you. You can then make a mental note of how the person responds and continue to adjust as needed moving forward.

Reflect On Your Highs and Lows

One of the most important principles of self-care and mental health is self-monitoring. To have good mental health, you have to engage in regular self-reflection. How else will you know what is going on internally or what needs your attention? For many Black men, self-reflection is not something we do frequently. Black boys are often rewarded for external and highly visible active behavior.

Focusing on what you can do (and what can be seen from the outside) is not wrong but often comes at the expense of developing a meaningful inner world. That means that little Black boys aren't rewarded in the same ways for sitting and thinking about their behavior, what makes them happy, or how they feel about things in general. In turn, these Black boys turn into grown Black men without much practice in how to name emotions and feelings, let alone share them with important people around them. If you've ever gotten the feedback that a loved one wants you to "share more," you likely fall into this group of men.

The good news is that the muscle of self-reflecting is developed much like any other muscle—by training and lots of practice. You can start this by simply taking time to reflect intentionally on your daily life. One of my favorite ways to do this is called Roses & Thorns.

The process is simple, and it's a way to reflect on your day by looking at both the good and the bad things that have happened. There's no prescription for how many good things (roses) you share or how many negative moments (thorns) you share. This may sound incredibly simple and it is, but what it allows you to do is very significant. With practice, this kind of reflection builds emotional intelligence. If you can routinely identify something as simple as what was good about your day, or not so good, a few things happen. You start to develop emotional nuance, broaden your vocabulary around feelings, and deepen your understanding of your own experiences. This allows you to practice vulnerability and emotional expression in a way that feels tangible, simple, and straightforward. That kind of vulnerability helps build relationships and improves your mental health by enabling you to have greater insight into the things that bother you and what you like about your life. Better communication empowers people in your life to support you with more clarity and understanding.

Take Action

Start by grabbing a notebook (or opening a note app on your phone) and writing out a few roses (good things) and thorns (frustrating or negative, etc., things) about your day. Examples of roses might be positive feedback from your colleague or something as simple as a delicious meal. Thorns may look like a frustrating meeting with your boss at work or getting into an argument with your partner. Try not to get hung up on whether what you come up with feels significant enough or life-changing. That's irrelevant. The most important thing is that you engage in the self-care practice to acknowledge your experience rather than just minimizing or ignoring it altogether. For best results, incorporate this practice into your daily routine. You might be surprised by how different you feel once you regularly give yourself space to honor your feelings.

Check Your Gas Tank

As a therapist, I often counsel clients on finding ways to engage in more routine personal check-ins because it enables you to notice subtle changes in your mood and energy levels. This can help you avoid waking up one day and realizing that things in your life have gotten out of control. You need to monitor your energy levels.

For far too long, Black men have internalized the myth that our bodies are all we have to offer to the world. This leads to increased stress and overworking. Black men need to do what's necessary to have the energy to do things for our families, our communities, and ourselves. One of the simplest ways to do this is to examine how your energy shifts daily, even from hour to hour.

One of my favorite, and straightforward, analogies for this is to think of yourself, or your energy level, as a gas tank. If you're into gaming, you might want to adopt the language of HP (hit points or health) or whatever your favorite game might call it. Regardless of the way you label it, this exercise is about taking a moment to determine how much energy you have and how much energy a recent activity has taken from you. In the gas tank analogy, you can consider being full of energy as having a full tank of gas. Conversely, feeling exhausted would be analogous to being close to an empty tank.

How does this help you day to day? If you permit yourself to check your fuel (or energy) levels throughout the day, you can make adjustments based on that information quickly. For example, if you're someone who drinks coffee regularly but somehow forgot to have your cup (or two), you're likely to feel very heavy and tired in the late morning. If you don't take a beat to check where your fuel level is, you might personalize, overthink why you're feeling so tired, and spend the rest of the day judging yourself. As a result, your work quality suffers, your mood shifts, and you feel irritable. This all could have been prevented if you had taken the time to investigate how you were feeling mid-morning and discovered that because your routine was off, you simply didn't have the caffeine you needed earlier. Checking in gives you the data you need to engage in self-care that makes sense for you on a practical level. Without that data, you're just wandering around feeling "off" and not really knowing why. No one deserves to feel that way.

Take Action

Where is your energy level right now? Are you feeling light and energized? Is your car a well-oiled machine, or are you feeling run-down and need some more fuel to get through the rest of your day? How would you go about getting that energy? Do you need to meet your basic needs of water and food, or do you need psychological or spiritual energy and inspiration? Once you take a moment to check in, you can get the answers that you need.

Develop a Sleep Routine

Getting good rest is one of the most important things you can do for your mental health. However, it's also one of the most often overlooked ways to practice self-care.

Many Americans struggle with some sort of sleep issue. Health conditions such as sleep apnea, restless leg syndrome, or insomnia are common. Restlessness is often a result of ongoing stress. And this is exacerbated when you don't have an established sleep routine. Sleep hygiene is a set of practices and conditions under which you're able to get restorative sleep. Poor sleep hygiene contributes to restlessness and poor sleep quality.

There are a few key steps in having good sleep hygiene, and they largely involve developing a solid routine. There are some general recommendations from organizations such as the Sleep Foundation: a dark bedroom, cooler indoor temperature, and little or no sound among them. You can also take that a step further and develop a more specific bedtime routine that includes things that are most helpful to you.

In developing your personalized routine, one matter you may want to consider is your overall wind-down routine (the things you do at the end of a workday). Do you often spend the time just before bed washing dishes or doing other chores that keep you up and moving? For some people, even these simple tasks can be activating and create a "busy" feeling rather than a relaxing one. If so, consider what action or inaction helps you wind down an hour or two before you want to be asleep. Common options are listening to soothing music, turning down lights, switching your phone to "do not disturb" mode, reading a book, and drinking sleep-enhancing tea. There are also many ways to create a more sleep-friendly bed. That could involve purchasing a special pillow that works better for side-sleepers or a new set of sheets that are more comfortable and cooler throughout the night. These are things Black men often overlook, but such minor details can make a big difference with getting quality rest.

Take Action

If you're struggling with getting good-quality rest, do a bit more research on sleep hygiene and figure out what practices or strategies could be most helpful for you. Develop a sound sleep routine to practice self-care and protect your physical and mental health and your acuity in the long run.

It can take some time to find and maintain a routine that works well for you. So, if you run into some restless nights as you try out different things, that's okay. You won't immediately find the perfect routine. Bad routines are not corrected *overnight*. Try out a few things before committing to any of them long term. If you continue to have trouble getting good rest after adopting some of the sleep hygiene recommendations, seek a licensed physician to determine whether you have a sleep disorder such as insomnia or sleep apnea.

Set Weekly Intentions

Self-determination is key to mental health.

Many years ago, I came across this statement and found that it perfectly encapsulates how important it is to move with intention for good mental health. But what does intention mean exactly? Intention is the idea that inspires your path forward. It is the energy that guides your behavior as you navigate some interaction or project. Intention is the "why" behind the steps you take to achieve something.

Most people move through life without intention as a constant guide. It's typically at only very specific times of the year—New Year's Eve, a birthday, an anniversary, and a job performance review among them—that most people make a conscious effort to think about how they might achieve their goals.

That kind of permission, and agency, is something that most Black folks haven't had the luxury of adopting. Faced with systemic discrimination, oppressed groups are more focused on staying financially afloat. For Black men, the focus on surviving in this socioeconomic system can reduce the urge to dream and pursue goals with intention. There's no judgment here if you've found yourself limited due to your personal circumstances.

If you've found yourself challenged by the system, you know how stifling it can be to live and act passively because of your focus on short-term needs. However, there may be some reasonable ways you can navigate your week more attuned to the steps you can take to gain control of your life and move through it with authenticity. For example, if your goal is to bring more of yourself to the workplace, then you may set a weekly intention of code-switching less at work. If your goal is to save money for your future home, then you may plan to order less takeout and cook more meals at home. Consider this a call to make some time to think about goals, daily steps to those objectives, and the joy of self-determination.

Take Action

This exercise is about taking your agency and power back. Make some time for quiet reflection and write down three ideas or steps that would enable you to advance toward your goals for each upcoming week. These are flexible and can always be updated if necessary. Don't feel pressured to get them perfectly right. While focusing on what you think you should be doing, you should also think about those intentions that feel deeply aligned. If it helps, you can also write an example or two of what behavior might help you embody those intentions daily for greater clarity and direction.

Try a Worry Dump

Like many other mental health concerns, anxiety is something that is often ignored in Black communities. This is especially true for most Black men. But, just like anyone else, Black men carry a lot of stress and need the opportunity to find space for catharsis and release of stress and anxiety in their lives.

For many Black men, anxiety is a foreign concept. In my work as a therapist, I've worked with many men who identify what anxiety feels like for them. As is often the case with many areas of mental health, most Black folks have never been given the education and language to best describe their emotional experiences. This, unfortunately, has contributed to the ongoing stigma of mental health and kept Black folks from getting much-needed support, especially when anxiety or worry causes disruptions in daily life.

Anxiety is often best described as either a psychological/mental or a physical experience, or both. Some people experience anxiety as thoughts that continue to occupy their minds—a racing internal monologue—despite their effort to focus on other things. Others experience anxiety as a physiological response that triggers physical reactions, such as increased heart rate, stomach issues, and shallow breathing. Most people experience a combination of the two, depending on the situation and the day.

Worry is an extension of anxiety; it is the experience of excessively dwelling on a concern. Worry is something that you often experience when trying to sleep at night. It can be difficult to "turn off" and rest when worry and anxiety have taken over. When you deal with concerns poorly, your brain can cycle on a hamster wheel of worry.

One tool that can help deal with worry is to write down all your thoughts and concerns on paper. Putting those concerns on paper helps externalize those thoughts, enabling you to get them out of your mind more easily. Writing out the thoughts can also help provide additional perspective. It's hard to realize how distorted thoughts can become when they only exist inside your head. Being able to read them aloud is a different kind of emotional processing that doesn't happen as readily if you only process them internally.

Take Action

Before you head to bed tonight, grab a notebook (or your phone) and write out all thoughts you're having a hard time avoiding. That's it! You don't have to do anything else with these thoughts. Just write them out, close your notebook or set aside your phone, and then move on. See if you feel any relief, either immediately or over time, with more practice.

If you continue to struggle with keeping anxious thoughts under control, you can also consult with a licensed therapist who can help you develop more personalized tools to feel more balanced and capable of focusing your time and energy on things you care about most.

Read Something New

Books can be portals to new perspectives as well as a source of self-care information. According to Pew Research, each year 27 percent of Americans do not read a single book. As a result of extremely busy schedules or the lack of interest in books, a fair amount of people miss out on the benefits of reading. Also, in schools, most of us were made to read things by authors on topics of little interest and irrelevant to our daily lives. This has been true for Black students because many schools still struggle to incorporate Black stories in their curriculum, largely because of ongoing efforts by conservatives to ban books that explore themes around race and racism, gender, and sexuality.

How can books be part of a self-care practice for Black men?

First, we must look at the intergenerational history of limiting the education of Black folks. The relationship between formal education and Black folks is complicated. In our history, Black thought leaders argued over whether Black people should invest in secondary education and higher learning or strictly invest in trade schools and other training opportunities. This was at the center of the discourse between Booker T. Washington and W.E.B. DuBois. Additionally, the relationship between reading and Black folks has largely been dictated by white folks. While white oppressors prohibited many enslaved Africans from reading throughout history, the intentional underfunding of public libraries and relevant attacks on books are modern-day methods for sustaining the racial education gap.

It's also important to consider the self-limiting stereotypes that influence Black reading habits. Black folks are still marginalized in certain genres. Also, there are few self-improvement books designed for African Americans. As a result, Black men have little access to new perspectives, and many need books that can help them improve emotional intelligence and relationships. Fiction has also been found to increase empathy. For example, when people read stories about characters who are different, they can relate and be transported to that fictional world. For a Black man who's looking for new perspectives, books are a relatively easy way to meaningfully engage with stories that differ from your own and develop more humility and empathy.

If you are someone who reads regularly, that's great. The challenge here is to dive into something new that you wouldn't typically read. Try a new author or a topic outside your experience. Use books to learn some new perspectives.

Take Action

Head to the bookstore or browse online and buy a book by an author with a different background and perspective. This might mean looking for authors who are from different racial or ethnic groups, books by people with disabilities, or stories that explore gender and sexuality differences that you don't encounter in your everyday life. Commit to reading the book you have chosen in the coming weeks.

Adjust Your Negative Thoughts

Many people struggle with negative thoughts, and it can be difficult to find a way to manage them.

Cognitive Therapy, a popular form of therapy, helps people identify and replace thoughts that are distorted or causing distress. At the core of this practice is challenging automatic thoughts. Most people deal with some form of distorted thoughts. We all have ways of looking at the world that may sometimes magnify negative experiences and over-personalize others. If you struggle with self-doubt and self-esteem, it might be more typical for you to have these kinds of thoughts directed at yourself. It's also common for people—especially Black men—to fail to recognize just how negative their internal monologue can be.

Negative thinking is common for people who struggle with reaching career goals or have other mental health issues that need treatment. It's also hard to think positively when the world around you continues to give you the message that who you are is less worthy than others. This is something that a lot of Black men can relate to as we often internalize messages about the ways we don't live up to other people's expectations. In this way, negative thinking is a reasonable response to the environment around you. However, there is a line between having negative thoughts and engaging in mental self-abuse. It is important to have tools and strategies to help manage the negative thoughts because they impact your mental health.

One of the ways people try to counter negative thoughts is by going too far in the opposite direction. That is when people try to chase away negative thoughts by envisioning themselves or their situations as ideal. They move from "I hate everything" to "Everything is perfect!" It is too far-fetched and disconnected from reality. To put it simply, try not to move from -10 thinking to +10 thinking. Instead, try to land on some thoughts that feel a little better than your original thinking but can still be reasonable and believable to you.

You might try thinking patterns that actually acknowledge both your current reality and your potential. For example, you can tell yourself: "I'm feeling dissatisfied with how things are going and need to change course." Can you see how a "positive" thought can be more reasonable and easier to believe? That's the point.

Take Action

Practice creating new and more believable positive thoughts on your own. Sometimes it's helpful to write down what you come up with so you can keep it at the front of your mind and revisit it often.

Changing how you think is hard work. If you're not used to adjusting your thoughts in this way, it's even more difficult to figure out where you need to land to make your alternative thought more believable. If you run into some trouble, that's normal. Like most things, you'll improve with practice. Give yourself time to adjust your thinking patterns.

Practice Daily Grooming

Most people take daily grooming for granted as an exercise in self-care. Showering, brushing your teeth daily, and grooming your hair are not just necessities but also opportunities to show yourself care and attention. Taking extra time to invest in taking care of your skin or trying a beard oil, for example, might feel silly when you're focused on so many other things. Black men, in particular, are often in such a preoccupied state because they are devalued and are the target of discrimination in greater society. As a result, grooming habits can feel low on your list of priorities. However, daily grooming can help you look good, feel good, and be healthier. It is an important aspect of self-care.

While there are no universal standards on how one should look, daily grooming often indicates how well someone is doing mentally and how capable they are of taking care of themselves. If you've ever experienced an episode of depression or dealt with a debilitating mental health condition, you have likely experienced difficulty in just getting through the day, let alone completing all your daily grooming habits. However, neglecting your daily grooming can also have negative outcomes for your health, including greater risk for illness, infection, and disease.

For health reasons, for example, brushing your teeth, showering regularly, and wearing clean and weather-appropriate clothes are hygiene-related grooming practices involved in self-care. Mental health professionals will first look at a patient's hygienic state when assessing a person's mental status. How we take care of ourselves reflects how we feel inside.

Daily grooming ensures that you're functioning at a normal and socially appropriate level of well-being. If you aren't taking good care of your hygiene and grooming, people will take notice, and such observations can have negative social and professional consequences. You may not even notice how far you've fallen behind or just how bad it has gotten until someone else points it out. It's never fun to receive that kind of feedback. This can generate a lot of shame and crush your confidence.

Excellent daily hygiene often communicates how well you are looking after yourself before you say a word. Routine haircuts, showering regularly, clipping your nails, and moisturizing daily make a positive impression on others. These are basic ways that show people around you that you care about your appearance and well-being. They also communicate confidence.

Daily grooming is a practical way to invest in yourself. You are worth the time and energy that daily grooming requires. No matter what styles you use to represent yourself, nothing is more important than being able to feel good in your skin because you've taken care of yourself and your most basic needs.

Take Action

If your personal grooming habits have fallen by the wayside due to stressors or other challenges in your life, this is your opportunity to restart. Take some time to get back to the basics—among them, showering, and brushing your teeth and your hair regularly.

Keep in mind that daily grooming is also a way to express your personality and style. In the long run, you'll feel a lot better. By caring for your appearance and hygiene, you can show up in the world as the best possible version of yourself. If you want to invest in new daily practices or products, a simple Internet search can help you explore new hairstyles, haircare practices, or proper care for your beard and skin from a Black man's perspective. Fortunately, there are more Black male content creators who also explore grooming as self-care these days. Even if you can't find the perfect source, give yourself permission to try something new and see if it works for you.

Make Amends

Sometimes the biggest barrier to healing is not giving yourself permission to do so. We don't talk enough about how burden lifting it can be to forgive yourself and make amends for something that you've done wrong.

Have you ever made a mistake and found yourself stuck in guilt and shame after realizing the negative impact you've had on someone else? In my experience as a therapist, this is common for many people, and it can keep you stuck in a path of self-criticism for a long time. For many Black men, in particular, we feel a lot of pressure to always be doing the right thing. When we falter, we easily fall into shame and self-criticism. Being stuck in this way can also create a self-fulfilling prophecy in which you personalize all future mistakes as evidence of just how messed up you are. This kind of shame negatively impacts your present and future as it leaks out in relationships, particularly in the face of criticism from a partner or loved one.

It's not hard to imagine why some people shut down when given feedback. In these moments, you're usually not just reacting to the moment at hand, you're also responding to your internal story about all the other mistakes you've made and what kind of person you must be. It's self-defeating and exhausting!

Every person in this world makes mistakes. Some of those mistakes are bigger than others. While it's reasonable to feel bad about making a mistake, there is a fine line between taking accountability for something that you've done and beating yourself up for a misstep. Some of us haven't had the process of taking accountability and apologizing modeled to us within our families, and we struggle with the vulnerability of doing so. Making amends is healing because it helps rid you of the guilt and shame that tend to eat away at people over time. This is the reason it's one of the principles of the Alcoholics Anonymous twelve-step program. Shame tends to thrive in silence. That means if you continue to feel shame about something you've done and you don't speak about that shame, forgive yourself, and make amends, shame will likely consume you from the inside out.

Working to forgive yourself and making apologies to the people you've wronged are important steps on a path toward healing.

Take Action

Your word is one of the strongest things you have to offer people in this world. When you go to make amends to someone, it is an acknowledgment of your accountability and wrongdoing, and that takes a lot of courage. While it can be nerve-racking or even scary to think about, the payoff is the possibility of true healing and maybe even reconciliation. This is your chance to turn a new page. If there's something you've done that you know is wrong, no matter how big or small, this is an invitation to move forward. Reach out to the person you've hurt and offer your sincere apology. Share with them how you'll prevent the undesired behavior from happening again. Once you're done, give yourself space to feel whatever feelings might have come up and process them with trusted allies or through more self-reflection, such as journaling.

Reach Out to a Friend

Loneliness is a hidden pandemic we need to address. Men, especially, are struggling to find the social and emotional support to feel grounded and balanced in today's society.

If the COVID-19 pandemic has taught us anything, it has shown us just how different our lives can be when we aren't able to spend time with people we love and care about. If you felt relatively unaffected by the distance between you and others throughout social distancing and isolation measures, then I'd like you to pay particular attention to this activity.

It would be incorrect to say that Black men don't have friendships. However, it is still more common than not that Black men do not feel satisfied with their level of social contact and support. It's in large part because Black men are not given tools to build meaningful and sustained relationships. Black men are often taught how to exist alongside other people, but not truly *with* others. Often, parents are largely focused on delivering two major key messages to Black boys: 1) come back home safely, and 2) get an education or find a job so that you can take care of yourself. This is all good but doesn't provide men with the tools necessary to create deep, fulfilling friendships.

As a result, Black men have a hard time accessing feelings of closeness and intimacy with other men in their lives. It's one thing to be "cool" with someone, but when was the last time you felt like you truly missed a friend that you haven't seen in a long time? Have you ever said that to a friend? This kind of experience, and language, is largely underused in Black male friendships.

Hopefully, other men mean something to you. Consider what author bell hooks so eloquently stated in her book *We Real Cool: Black Men and Masculinity*: "At the center of the way Black male selfhood is constructed in white supremacist capitalist patriarchy is the image of the brute—untamed, uncivilized, unthinking, and *unfeeling"* (emphasis added). Being able to have meaningful relationships, be they romantic or platonic, is key to mental health. Human beings are social creatures. Given the state of the world and the battles against racism and prejudice you must wage, you likely need more support than you think. This means taking a step to deepen the friendships you already have.

Take Action

Your challenge is to reach out to a friend that you haven't spoken to in a while. You can call just to catch up or set up some plans to meet soon. Intentionally reconnect and work toward making platonic relationships a priority in your life. If you have a friend who you appreciate, try to deepen the friendship by talking about stuff that matters to you or issues you are trying to resolve. Many Black men don't have trusted sources of meaningful emotional support. Your brother might be wanting and needing that kind of space with you too.

Respond to a Microaggression

Microaggressions are the interpersonal slights you encounter every day. These are the statements that tend to play on prejudicial thoughts and stereotypes of a marginalized group. I wonder if you have heard some overzealous white person say, "You speak so articulately!" Or perhaps someone has told you how "big" you must be because you're a Black man. These comments are so commonplace these days that many people have come to accept them as fact. And they can be subconscious or intentional on the part of the offender.

But, like any other group, Black men need not be reduced to simple, and outdated, stereotypes even if they are sometimes positive. You do not have to continue to subject yourself to these kinds of microaggressions.

It's important to acknowledge that when you use your voice to counteract microaggressions, you are also standing up to help defend the greater community of Black men. Standing up in this way is both self-care and community care. More responses are needed because these kinds of statements have persisted for long enough already. It's reductive and dehumanizing. You deserve better than that.

Responses should be tailored for different types of microaggression. Some of these transgressions might seem benign. For example, tokenism can be expressed as unwarranted high praise. This kind of comment generates a feel-good moment for the speaker, but they insult the intelligence of Black men. "Why do you talk like that or speak so loud?" might be a more overt example. Regardless of intention, these incidents negatively impact our mental health. Feeling confused about how to respond exacerbates the negative feelings. It's important that you find a way to stand up for yourself in these moments.

You have options when it comes to responding in moments like these. How you respond is influenced by the environment, your relationship with the offender, and your comfort level in being assertive, among other things. There is no right or wrong way to respond.

Hopefully, the offending person takes your feedback to heart and challenges their prejudicial thoughts. At the very least, it might help deter offenders from expressing those kinds of comments to other Black men. I think it's fair to consider that responses that prompt offenders to self-check their behavior are wins.

Take Action

The next time you're faced with a microaggression during a conversation, consider the benefits and risks of addressing things head-on. Any confrontation requires emotional energy, so it's okay to take time to decide whether it makes sense for you to respond.

If you do respond, be clear and concise in what's problematic about the comment and offer the correction. It's the best way to promote awareness, and it increases the odds that these verbal offenses will occur less often. You can deflect with a humorous response that rebuts their comments. Or, if the situation involves more blatant racial references, you could be blunter in your response. If necessary, you could also call in others, such as associates, to discuss the issue. It's up to you to choose. While it's not your responsibility to educate, it is up to you to set limits on problematic behavior as an act of self-care.

Try Meditation

Meditation is not for everyone, and that's okay. But it does offer a tangible way to practice spirituality, even in its most secular forms. And if spirituality isn't something that you want to work on in this way, then meditation and breath work also allow you to connect more with your body, which can be very helpful in your self-reflection efforts. Meditation has been found to produce relaxation and increase focus. In addition, meditation is shown to improve heart health and reduce blood pressure. Those benefits can be of special value to Black men, who can have higher levels of cardiovascular strain than other ethnic groups and genders.

On a simpler level, meditation can provide you with a space and time to connect with yourself to take better care of yourself. As you get more connected to your body, you gain deeper insight into your internal experiences, such as thoughts, feelings, and sensations. This knowledge helps you gain clarity on what you're feeling, what your desires or needs may be, and what next steps might be helpful to take in your life. Whether you're dealing with relationship issues or difficulties with your manager at work, or trying to cope with the ongoing injustices against Black folks around the globe, meditation provides a healing space for you.

There is a steep learning curve with meditation, and this can be a barrier for a lot of people. Meditation is considered a *practice* for that reason. In its simplest forms, meditation may give you guided directions for a breathing practice. Its more advanced forms might involve you focusing on reciting a key phrase or a mantra for an extended period. It requires a great deal of discipline. Another key benefit of meditation is the enhanced ability to develop the patience and discipline required to focus on the present moment.

Some people find it too difficult to sit in one place and meditate for fifteen minutes or longer. However, there are a lot of helpful resources for people who want to give meditation a try. There are digital apps and online classes—many of them free. These guided meditations usually range from five to thirty minutes.

Take Action

Give meditation a try! You don't have to feel pressured to meet certain expectations, such as specific seating positions, hand poses, extended times, etc. If you're new to the practice, try shorter guided meditations initially to get a feel for what it's like.

Try not to be discouraged if you find your mind wandering or distracted. Distractions are part of the process and what people call "monkey mind," a state involving scattered and restless thinking. Treat yourself with compassion by giving yourself time to meditate effectively and keep it going. Give it a few tries before you decide if you like it or not, especially if it's difficult for you to feel good at something completely new.

Set a Boundary

Boundaries seem to be a hot topic these days and for good reason. Most of us are overwhelmed with news and commentary online. We have trouble managing relationships. Also, social media is demanding that we share more and more of our private lives. We need to set parameters that protect us and our loved ones for the sake of our mental health.

A boundary is a space in which you can care for yourself and another person simultaneously. For example, if you're annoyed by a friend who you think complains too much, you might create a healthy boundary by making him or her aware of this, by asking the friend why that is or to limit complaining, and by asking your friend how you can help him or her be more present in fun moments. Setting a boundary, or communicating a limit, doesn't need to look like ignoring or avoiding someone completely.

There are different qualities of boundaries. Some boundaries are porous and easily crossed. In the example of the boundary with a friend who complains too much, if the boundary is porous, you may feel disrespected if your friend takes advantage of the fact that you are not firm on this boundary. Overly porous boundaries can be harmful because they do not block out the impact of the negative behavior of others. If that boundary crossing comes from a friend, you are not helping by staying silent about it.

At the other end of the spectrum are boundaries that are too rigid. For example, your friend may feel unable to talk to you about anything difficult going on in their life if you have set a very rigid boundary around complaining. These kinds of boundaries make people unreachable and disconnected.

There are also more manageable healthy boundaries between these two extremes. When it comes to relationships that do not involve abuse, aim for a sturdy yet flexible approach. The healthy boundaries in the middle of the porous and rigid extremes allow contact and exchange of information and emotions between people—but with reasonable limits. Asking your friend to complain less and helping them to resolve any lingering issues, if they need help, can be an example of a healthy boundary. If that doesn't work, you may opt to spend less time with them, for now. That can also be a healthy boundary.

Black men, in particular, are not frequently taught about the large middle ground when it comes to boundaries. Instead, we often oscillate between the two extremes. On one hand, we allow whatever to happen so we can be *good* friends, partners, brothers, etc., becoming overwhelmed as a result. On the other hand, we shut down friends or potential friends by setting very rigid boundaries. For most situations, neither is the best option. Setting and maintaining healthy boundaries takes quite a bit of trial and error.

Take Action

Think about the state of your relationships right now. Have you been feeling satisfied with how your friends, partner, or family members engage with you? Are you happy with the boundaries you've been implementing with people in your life? What would you like to change? Brainstorm ways to communicate your concerns and aim for that healthy balance that will help you maintain the relationship but also empower you to practice self-care at the same time.

Limit Your Alcohol Intake

Over the past few decades, more research has been conducted on the impact of alcohol on our health. Out of that research, one conclusion is that moderate drinking has some health benefits, but there is still so much that we do not know about alcohol's impact on long-term health. Given that, there's a reason for everyone—especially African-American men and Black boys—to be cautious.

A 2018 study by Euchay Ngozi Horsman at the University of Arkansas shows that for Black male youth, in particular, early alcohol use increases the risk for Alcohol Use Disorder, a substance abuse diagnosis, at four times greater than their white counterparts. We now know that the previously reported health benefits of light drinking may have been overstated. Also, recent research suggests that even light-to-moderate drinking (1–2 drinks per day) may offer no meaningful benefit in preventing coronary heart disease. In addition, the reported health benefits may have been due to other healthy lifestyle factors in folks who generally tend to drink less.

It's a commonly accepted idea that what you put in your body impacts your overall health and how you feel. Thankfully, Black communities are becoming more aware of this and continue to advocate for healthier food access and food justice, particularly in low-income or urban communities, which suffer from a lack of supermarkets. Additionally, alcohol is big business, particularly in the United States. Advertising often intentionally targets young Black men, and younger people overall, reinforcing a party lifestyle that normalizes binge drinking.

That's not to say that you can't enjoy alcohol as an adult. For most people, alcohol use is largely social and offers some personal pleasure that doesn't cause any easily noticeable negative health impact.

However, it's important to be very mindful of the negative impact of advertising and the positive impact of reading peer-reviewed research and health reports when you are considering what is "normal" or healthy to put in your body. Whether you're thinking about alcohol consumption or any other health news, it's always important to be a critical—and maybe even skeptical—consumer and ask, "Who benefits most from this report or finding?" Drinking alcohol is one of the last areas that need to be mindfully addressed considering the lingering questions about how it impacts health in the long term.

Take Action

Take an inventory of your relationship with alcohol. How many days per week do you consume any alcohol? How much do you drink each time, and how do you typically feel after drinking? How do you feel the day after? For many Black men, alcohol is something that brings ease and comfort at the end of a long day. It can be part of a relatively healthy wind-down routine. However, many of us learned during the COVID-19 pandemic that alcohol can easily become a crutch when you're feeling low and don't have other outlets to cope. Even if you don't end your consumption, remember that the research is clear that less alcohol is better for your overall health. If you find yourself concerned about your consumption, seek a licensed mental health provider to help you redefine your relationship to alcohol and find what works for you.

Make SMART Goals

It can be incredibly frustrating when you're trying to reach a personal goal and just can't seem to cross the finish line. Unfortunately, when we get stuck in a rut and frustrated, it becomes relatively easy for our mental health to suffer as self-criticism creeps in. Practical tools can help.

Black men are under a lot of pressure to achieve. Some of this pressure comes from the family and the greater culture at large, as well as heavy internal pressure to follow through for yourself. That pressure can be crippling as it adds up over time. It's also normal to lose focus and momentum when other life issues steal your time and energy.

Simple strategies can help create the structure needed for your success. SMART goal-setting offers a helpful framework to help you decide how to reach your goals and discern what's reasonable to aim for in the first place. SMART is an acronym that stands for the following:

- **Specific:** This means creating a goal that clearly outlines your desired goal or objective. For example, rather than saying, "I want to take better care of my mental health," you might say instead, "I will start weekly therapy to take care of my mental health."

- **Measurable:** Your goal is best when it's easily measurable and observable. Measurable goals are easy to determine by some objective measure. Using the prior example, going to therapy weekly is measurable, as you can easily tell whether you attend a session. "I'll go to therapy often" is abstract and relative.

- **Attainable:** To be successful at achieving your goal, you will need to choose something that's reasonably attainable. For example, you won't be able to go to therapy weekly if the fee is too high for your budget. When you need to, negotiate and problem-solve to make the goal possible.

- **Relevant:** You can only achieve goals that are meaningful and relevant to your life. In essence, it's critical to understand your "why" and how this goal fits into the greater story of your life. Without meaning and purpose, it will be hard to find inspiration and motivation when you're not feeling your best.

- **Timely:** You give yourself a defined deadline and set up a clear schedule if it's something that requires ongoing work.

Take Action

Now that you better understand what SMART goals are, it's your turn to make some that work for you. Get out a notebook and jot down a few ideas for how you would like your life to improve. These could be health, professional, or even relationship goals. Once you have a couple of ideas to work with, write down the acronym "SMART" beneath them and determine if each goal meets the SMART criteria discussed. If not, what changes can you make?

When you determine they meet the SMART criteria, add those goals to your to-do list, calendar, or electronic reminders to help you stay on track. Every little bit helps, and these kinds of tools can help set you up for success.

Make an Active Coping Plan

How do you cope with stress in your life? Coping is the process of how we deal with and manage our responses to the world around us. Coping is how you react to your experiences, hopefully in a way that feels healthy and productive for you. People often cope passively. That is, they don't recognize what they do to deal with the worries and stresses of their life. They do things automatically and without thinking. In my experience, many Black men operate with this mentality, likely because we haven't been taught any other way. Many of us grew up with some version of "Just keep your head down and keep working." There is another way.

Active coping includes the following steps: 1) identifying your feelings and honoring the experience of what happened to you, and 2) responding to those feelings with targeted strategies and skills to help soothe yourself at that moment. What makes active coping so powerful is that it enables you to intentionally address whatever pain point has just been hit. Active coping is not throwing strategies at your pain and hoping something hits the mark.

As an example, many people are struggling with loneliness and isolation. You might feel that yearning to have someone to talk to or go with to your favorite restaurant. Maybe you want someone you can trust with your frustrations. What might you do about that? Some find it too difficult to locate people to reach out to or trust that they will help them feel better. Instead of making that call, they may distract themselves from their feelings by binge-watching streaming shows, drinking, or smoking until they can zone out. That's coping and sometimes it works! It's not a particularly healthy way of coping for two reasons: Those ways aren't sustainable and may cause other issues when overused, and they don't actually address the core issue at hand, which, in this case, is isolation.

It may sound very simple, but a more active way of coping with loneliness would be to actually connect with another person. Active coping, in this example, would mean reaching out to a friend via text or call, connecting with people you game with online, or even making a plan to meet up with someone in person in the future. These options help you feel more connected, as they actively address, and resolve, feeling alone. That's what active coping is about—using an appropriate, individualized, and productive response to target the undesired feeling or emotion.

Take Action

How are you feeling right now? Is there some feeling or experience you're having that feels more negative than positive? If so, now is a good time to brainstorm some ideas about how you can actively cope and not just distract yourself. If you're feeling good at the moment, this is an excellent time to plan for the future. Think back to the last time you felt frustrated, isolated, etc., and plot out some options for new ways to cope next time. Target the feeling's core with concrete action steps. Save the list on your phone, or somewhere easily accessible, so the next time you struggle, you already have a blueprint for how you can practice better self-care.

Take a Nap

"At the end of the day, for us to imagine a new world, a new world that centers liberation, equality, and justice, rest is going to have to be our center foundation. We will not be able to create these new inventive ways of being from an exhaustive state, and that goes to abolition."
—Tricia Hersey

Tricia Hersey, the founder of The Nap Ministry, is on a message mission. Her message: "Rest is Resistance." Hersey, a performance artist, says the intergenerational trauma of slavery and Jim Crow is still with us today because the descendants of the enslaved have adverse emotional and behavioral reactions to that collective horror. That includes stress that often impedes the ability to get regular, refreshing sleep. This message should resonate with Black men. You need more rest.

Black men in America have been dehumanized, deemed expendable creatures, and revered and feared for perceived physical strength and endurance. You and I both know that you are more than that. However, it's not far-fetched to conclude that you may have internalized this view of Black men. Simply put, identifying with the stereotypical image makes it difficult for you to allow yourself to rest.

There's a long history in the United States of prizing physical accomplishments and abilities of Black folks over anything else. Enslaved Africans, our ancestors, were forced to endure immeasurable pain through forced servitude. Our ancestors were bonded, raped, murdered, and lynched all for the sake of helping white people achieve their dream of "life, liberty, and the pursuit of happiness." Happiness for whom, though?

Science has shown that this pain and intergenerational trauma can be encoded into your DNA. There is a constant desire and need to prove your worth and productivity. This is only exacerbated by rigorous expectations of capitalism. Many Black men—and Black women as well—have embraced the so-called capitalistic work ethic to the extent that they associate rest with laziness. Furthermore, devotion to "the grind" is choking the entire culture. Pair that with every systemic and individual bias you encounter in your life, along with everyday stressors, and I bet you are exhausted. It's okay to acknowledge this. This is your sign. This is your opportunity to acknowledge that it's okay to rest.

Take Action

Your challenge is to take action by embracing inaction. If you're not a napper, allow your body to rest without the expectation of doing anything else. This is easier said than done when you have the programming of capitalism in your head along with your actual needs to make ends meet and take care of yourself and your family. But remember that you can do all that. You can be the man that you want to be *and* you can make time to let your body and spirit embrace the kind of rest that your ancestors were denied. Rest is your birthright. Permit yourself to lay your head and worries down for just a few moments. Your health demands it.

Embrace Your Softness

From the earliest days of their youth, Black boys are prepared for manhood. This gets in the way of Black men getting to experience life as Black boys.

While nicknames such as "Little Man" are terms of endearment in the Black community, they are also symbolic of community efforts to accelerate the maturation of Black boys. This kind of protection is necessary and helpful in our world, but it also has unintentional consequences.

Black children are often thought of as more mature and aggressive compared to their white counterparts. This is a form of implicit bias that we have for Black children and darker-skinned people around the globe. We easily attribute negative attributes to darker-skinned folks, and this creates a dynamic in which darker-skinned people are most vulnerable. Black folks have tried to prepare their boys for this reality by hardening them. We readily emphasize the strength, speed, and aggression of Black boys to help them survive in the world. However, that leaves their emotional sensitivities underdeveloped.

Saying the word "soft" to a Black man is thought of as a slur. Maybe you've called someone else that, or perhaps it's a word that's been hurled at you to make you feel smaller and less of a man. This is an example of that hardening that Black men are exposed to from a young age. Receiving this message repeatedly creates a belief that Black men (and boys) are by nature hard and strong. What happens to the gentleness, affection, and love that a Black boy would like to express? We teach him those traits aren't valued. He's taught that his feelings are liabilities while navigating the world. He becomes disconnected from those softer parts of himself, and as he ages, he forgets those parts are natural and exist in the deepest parts of his soul.

These messages are not only reinforced in many Black homes but also in society's representations of what it means to be Black and male. For example, consider the many movies involving action-oriented and sometimes violent Black characters and the lack of films featuring sensitive Black men who are in touch with their feelings.

To counter this, we must connect to Black masculinity in its full complexity. Black men are strong. You have your ancestors to thank for the power of resilience that runs through your veins. However, Black men are also tender and loving partners and nurturing fathers. Black men are capable of the entire range of human emotion. You can honor your feelings and be responsive to the emotions of people around you. That rests on the ability to connect with the side that feels "soft" and vulnerable.

Take Action

There are many ways to embrace the softer, more emotional side of you. It could involve sharing something that's been on your mind with someone close to you. Reach out to friends and listen to them. Model this softness by hugging your Black son and telling him that you love him, no matter how old he is. Tell a loved one that you're struggling with something and need their support. Step outside of your comfort zone and see how it feels to embrace this part of you more often. That is healing.

Revisit a Dream Deferred

In his poem "Harlem," Langston Hughes poses a question about what happens to a *dream deferred* (one that is put aside again and again, unfulfilled). Ultimately, he proposes this dream ends up being a heavy load for us—or it ends up crumbling altogether. We have to ask ourselves, "What is the cost of not dreaming?"

"Harlem" is all about the Black pursuit of racial equality and what happens when that dream is continuously deferred. It's a powerful message that reflects the depth of pain many Black folks still experience as the fight for justice continues. For Black men, dreams deferred are a deeply personal experience. Have you ever had a plan for your life that, for whatever reason, never materialized? Have your own actions or the circumstances of life placed barriers in your way despite your best attempts to achieve the goal?

As rich and empowering as it can be to live as a Black man in this world, it can also be incredibly challenging. Societal and individual barriers might keep you from reaching your highest heights. This causes a sense of deep frustration and sadness for Black men. Whether those barriers are structural (such as racism) or more personal (needing to shift career plans due to family or financial needs), it is incredibly hard to watch your dreams float away. We don't talk about the pain of this kind of loss enough.

However, dreaming is a revolutionary act and represents hope personified. For Black men, the path toward making that dream a reality can be harder for us than it is for others. Not being able to reach the goals you set for yourself can leave you feeling hopeless and resigned to a life that isn't up to your own standards.

Sometimes this kind of mindset shift is necessary to make ends meet and take care of yourself or your family. Permitting ourselves to dream and hope is also part of the healing that we need as Black men. As we tend to overemphasize the practical, it can be easy to forget there can be more to life than what is right in front of us. What happens when you don't dare to dream? It means you stop trying to improve yourself and your life.

Take Action

There is energy and power in possibility. Take some time to revisit a dream or personal goal that has fallen by the wayside over the years. Maybe you gave up a creative outlet because it didn't feel practical enough. Or you gave up on furthering your education because it felt impossible at the time. Determine, if you can, specifically what prevented you from realizing the goal. Was it finances or other life circumstances that prevented you from reaching your goal? Was it the internalizing of a lot of messaging from people around you that destroyed your confidence? Could there be the possibility of reconnecting to this dream and making it a part of your life now? Permit yourself to explore what role this goal can have in your life now compared to when you conceived the dream. Be flexible in your analysis and imagining. Instead of telling yourself the goal isn't possible, try to think of the steps you can take to achieve it. Odds are that will help you feel a lot freer and at peace.

Heal a Father Wound

For as long as I can remember, people have been saying, "That's because she has daddy issues." It's about time that we acknowledge the fact that men have "daddy issues" too. That can be especially true for Black men.

The relationship between a father and son is one of the most important relationships any boy has. It is the foundation upon which a boy learns to first understand himself. If a father is present in those early years, it is the first model of what masculinity looks like. For a young boy, watching your father navigate your family and the world around him is like looking into a crystal ball. Unconsciously, the father represents the living embodiment of your future. He is the primary symbol of what it means to be a man.

Black fathers have a profound impact on the lives of their children. Maybe this is something you will also come to learn should you become a father in the future (or perhaps you have already become one).

Black men, including Black fathers, haven't historically been afforded a wide range of ways to show up in the world. Being a "good provider" is one culturally specific story that continues to predominate ideas about modern parenthood. These days, however, expectations are expanding. Today, more Black men declare that their value is not just their role as financial providers. More and more, you are expected to provide emotional support to family and friends. That's difficult if you're mired in grief about past discrimination and trauma.

While some fathers were always conscious about being present in this kind of way, many Black fathers didn't have the time, space, or *skills* to lovingly demonstrate more relational support. If you add on the pressures of navigating multiple systems of oppression such as underemployment, mass incarceration, and financial subjugation,

Black fathers of a certain time were still largely preoccupied with doing what seemed necessary for survival. Black fatherhood is a particular kind of beast for this reason. It is also a gift.

Within this context, many Black boys grew up with physically or emotionally absent fathers. This lack of warmth and presence is so easily felt, particularly in young Black boys who are trying to find and understand their place in the world. But how you can begin to formulate a deep understanding of the joys and difficulties of navigating life as a Black man if you needed more help, more conversations, and more presence from your own father?

Take Action

The experiences of Black families are not monolithic. As a therapist, I have learned that regardless of how good a parent is, there is almost always a gap between what a child wanted or needed and what the parent could give. This is not an indictment of parenthood or Black fathers but more so a recognition of the complexity of the parent-child relationship. Take some time today to identify what you felt like you were missing or needed more of from your father growing up. Consider what wounds you may be carrying and explore ways to respond to them with renewed insight. Do you need to respond to yourself with more compassion and care to heal because you missed out on that from your father? Do you need to take some small risks in sharing your feelings with a trusted friend because you find it difficult to trust others? If you have trouble coming up with ways to respond to these wounds, consider talking to a professional for more insight and guidance.

Get to Know Your Shadow

Sometimes self-care for many Black men can look like a straightforward strategy or skill, and sometimes it can require digging a bit deeper. That is the case with shadow work.

If you're unfamiliar with shadow work, it is a concept created by psychoanalyst Carl Jung. In his theories to best understand the fullness of human psychology, Jung believed that every person has a hidden side, which he called the shadow. The shadow represents the darker parts of ourselves or the parts of ourselves that have become repressed. This is due to how difficult these things can be to face. Jung believed things such as personal imperfections, pain, and trauma reside in the shadow side of the psyche. These parts being hidden or largely unconscious means they often are unconscious drivers of our thoughts and behaviors and create a sense of internal pain and conflict when unaddressed.

Jung believed that with intentional work such as meditation and journaling practices, anyone could gain access to their shadow material and work on healing and accepting those parts through a process called *individuation* or, as I like to call it, *integration*. That means if you can acknowledge these deeper, hidden parts of yourself and work toward accepting them with self-compassion, you can be more in touch with yourself and lead a more peaceful life.

Shadow work offers you an opportunity to look at yourself through a lens of radical self-compassion. Whether you have thoughts rooted in self-criticism or revenge fantasies, you are still deserving of the care and compassion that you extend to the people around you.

Jung theorized that everyone has a bit of a dark side they hide from the rest of the world and even from themselves. This means you're not alone if you're not sure why your thoughts tend to be negative for no *apparent* reason. Too often, people shame themselves for thoughts they have. But it is important to remember there is a big difference between fantasizing about something dark and actually engaging in behavior that is malicious or harmful (which is not okay). These kinds of thoughts do not necessarily lead to this kind of behavior. Identifying your shadow material can help you better understand yourself and pave the way for improved emotional health.

Take Action

It's not easy to reflect on the parts of yourself that you'd much rather keep hidden, and sometimes it is difficult to even access deeply stored thoughts, memories, or traumas. If you need support with this kind of work, you can reach out to a therapist to help you explore these ideas in a safe, supportive environment. Or you can do the work with the help of a reflection-based journal or book, such as my book, *The Shadow Work Workbook*.

Engage In Meaning-Making

At this stage in life, you have likely had a range of experiences, both good and bad, and found ways to keep moving forward. Sometimes, as Black men, it is easy for us to experience something difficult and keep our heads down to forge ahead. We may not stop to even acknowledge our pain, let alone create meaning from it. Yet we should do this because meaning-making is a powerful mental health tool.

Meaning-making can be one of the most enlightening psychological forces you have in life. However, the expression "meaning-making" is not well-known—not even among those who engage in the practice. Many don't know meaning-making when they hear it. For example, the saying "It was just God's will" is an example of meaning-making. If you look at the spirit of the saying, it's safe to assume that the goal is to give meaning to an otherwise challenging experience. That is, it means to say, "This pain that you're feeling right now is also in service of something else. There is more to this experience than your pain."

Again, it's not perfect, but once you dig deeper, it does feel different, doesn't it?

Meaning-making helps us find the purpose we need after a traumatic experience. Holocaust survivor Viktor Frankl explores ideas around resiliency and meaning-making in his book *Man's Search for Meaning*. It's become one of the most important texts from the twentieth century for helping people who have survived unimaginable pain and loss. Frankl himself lost several members of his own family throughout his time in concentration camps. His experiences furthered his previous work as a researcher on depression and suicide.

While it is not helpful to always look for a silver lining in life's most painful moments, it can be helpful to explore what meaning or role that pain holds for life ahead. Pain can be overwhelming. It can be especially difficult to manage when you don't think you have the support or resources to help guide you through it. It's common to become trapped in that hurt until making it out no longer feels tenable. But meaning-making can help you look at your experiences with a focus on the future. It gently points you toward a life that includes your experience but is not halted by it. Meaning-making allows for a sense of personal control and agency as you decide how you want to live with a painful experience.

Take Action

Take a moment now to reflect on an experience that brought you anxiety or pain. Imagine how this experience can inform your life moving forward. Is there something you can take from the experience aside from the pain? Is there some meaningful message about your own strength or resiliency that can provide you with hope for the future?

Take a Trip (Maybe Even Solo)

Even in a rapidly changing world, travel is still one of the most common ways in which people find relief, reduce stress, and learn more about themselves. For Black men, traveling can be both an enriching and a nerve-racking experience.

You may or may not be someone who likes to travel. If you are, you probably have no problem dreaming of your next places to visit as you add to the travel fund for your next trip. However, if you have not experienced the joys of traveling, this activity is an invitation to understand how it can change your life.

Travel can be a huge expense and a privilege that shuts out many people. The concerns around this magnify if you're a primary breadwinner in your home or work in an environment that makes it all but impossible to take time off. Due to financial issues alone, traveling can feel like a silly expense for many. However, it's time to also consider it as an investment in your health and well-being.

Research has shown that travel for pleasure can reduce stress and help us detach from work and the challenges of everyday life. Even a short weekend trip can do wonders for your mental health and your ability to find satisfaction in life. This means you don't have to break the bank to make a getaway to a new culture or to have a unique experience—even if it's simply a trip to a local town you've never visited. Also, don't be afraid to travel alone. It can be liberating to do what you want to do on your own time. By traveling, you can learn a lot about yourself—including what makes you feel giddy or nervous. Via travel, you have the opportunity to challenge yourself to adapt to new situations in faraway places or closer to home.

For Black men, travel offers a specific opportunity to engage in their world and environment differently. Anti-Blackness has been globalized. However, Black people are perceived a variety of ways around the world—and that perception is positive in many places.

If you never take the opportunity to travel to new places, you can miss out on what it feels like to experience the world differently. This can be scary, of course, and every Black person needs to be conscious about "Sundown Towns"—yes, there are some "no-Blacks-after-dark" communities abroad. However, if you do your homework, you can identify places where Black people are welcomed and valued.

It's not uncommon for people to come back from a trip with a new understanding of other cultures and great memories of beautiful scenery and tasty cuisine. Traveling is enriching for the mind and spirit. Also, once you travel for pleasure, you will want to do it more, according to Chen and Patrick. The researchers identified three factors of travel benefits—experiential excitement, health, and relaxation—and concluded that such experiences prompt people to travel more.

Take Action

If you're contemplating a trip, why not take the opportunity now to solidify some plans? If you haven't yet decided on a place to go, think about the kinds of places that might interest you. Next, do the research necessary to find places where you will be welcome. If English is not the common language in the land you are planning to visit, take time to learn some of the basic expressions in that country's language. Finally, develop an itinerary that fits your lifestyle and budget.

Take Yourself on a Date

When was the last time you took yourself on a date? For men—especially Black men—it can be difficult to identify activities that will enable you to help move the needle toward feeling good and grounded. Self-care can include many activities you may not have thought of before. One of the most impactful can be taking yourself on a date.

It's not a waste of money to invest in yourself this way. There's a reason women prioritize downtime—whether it's spending time with friends or spending some time window-shopping on their own. It gives them time to step away from their responsibilities and do something that's simply *for them.* Of course, Black men have their own desired activities, and they tend to look a little different, but there is something to be said for making it a point to treat yourself the way you treat someone you love. Why not do that for yourself too?

Maybe you're not the kind of man who appreciates getting dressed up and having a "nice" dinner, and that's okay. That doesn't have to be your plan. However, much like planning a date with someone else, you want to do something that is fun and out of the ordinary. That means watching football or movies at home late into the night doesn't quite get at what you're trying to do here. Try stepping outside of your comfort zone.

Taking yourself on a date might involve going to a bookstore, making a purchase, or having a quiet coffee alone. Or it could be a night at a concert by a recording artist who doesn't appeal to your partner, friends, or family. Dating yourself could also be a walk around a local park and treating yourself to ice cream afterward as you people-watch. Whatever it is, it's about doing something that's not quite in your everyday routine—but is still something enjoyable or exciting. As they say, "The world is your oyster." What can you do with it?

Take Action

Permit yourself to step outside of the norms and stereotypes associated with you and do something that you've always wanted to do instead of waiting until you can find someone to join you.

This is a good time to experiment. Do something you think you would enjoy, like a new activity. This is your time to do something that's just for you. It may be unusual for you to go solo, but ultimately, you will have the opportunity to spend the day with good company: yourself.

Permit Yourself to Grieve

Grief and loss are universal experiences. To be well and embrace healing, we have to make space for grief in our lives. Black people live with so much grief. Not only do we have to live with grieving the greater social justice challenges, but we also carry the personal weight of grief for those we've lost along the way.

Grief is a difficult experience for anyone—especially for Black men who don't have many spaces that feel safe enough to lean into that grief. In our society, there is a pressure associated with trying to "move on" after losing someone. For some Black men, this stigma associated with grief offers an escape hatch for facing the depth of our feelings and refocusing on providing for our families. "Moving on" can be an attempt to ignore the reality that when you lose someone you love, you are never the same person again. But the truth is that you cannot simply move on from that grief. You have to learn to live alongside it because that grief will always be with you in some form or fashion.

For Black men, grieving can be particularly difficult because it forces us to be in touch with our deepest feelings. Grieving is about honoring the intimacy and closeness of a relationship—whether it's familial, platonic, or romantic—and the reality that the relationship cannot continue. We can experience that grief because of a rift in our family, a breakup with a partner, or an actual physical death. While each of these types of loss has its own healing process, grieving offers you the opportunity to make meaning of the loss and determine how you need to honor your loss moving forward.

How can you begin to open your heart to grief when all the messages you've received throughout your life equate expressions of sadness with weakness? In the wake of a loss, how often have you heard, "You need to be strong!" That pressure to be "strong" in the face of grief does nothing but squash the love that grief allows us to feel.

Losing someone is incredibly hard and painful. You can cycle through the stages of grief forever, ranging from rage to a deep sadness that feels as if it will not relent. Grief can evolve. It can shrink or take on new meaning and generate different feelings as we move throughout life, but it never leaves. It just changes. Either way, everyone deserves space to honor a loss in whatever way that enables them to connect with the pain instead of trying to avoid it. This is the work of grieving. You deserve the space for this too.

Take Action

There are many ways to honor your grief. If someone you love has passed away, maybe you might take some time to visit their final resting place. Or you might write them a letter updating them on your life since they left and how much you miss them. You may even spend some time perfecting one of their signature recipes or sending up a prayer for them. Perhaps you will try all these and then some. The most important thing you can do right now is to give yourself the space to feel the depth of your feelings without self-judgment or self-criticism.

Try Forest Bathing

Much like mindful walking, forest bathing can help promote better mental health and is a relatively easy way to practice self-care.

Forest bathing was first defined in 1982 by Japan's Ministry of Agriculture, Forestry, and Fisheries. Shinrin-yoku (forest bathing) is the practice of mindfulness in a forest environment while strolling trails, exercising in that natural environment, or simply meditating. In contrast to the overly stimulated environment that most of us experience daily, forest bathing offers a time to reconnect with oneself by using the five senses (touching, hearing, smelling, seeing, and tasting).

As a self-care approach, forest bathing has a host of physical and psychological benefits.

For example, forest bathing has been found to reduce overall stress levels. Also, an analysis of more than twenty-eight studies on the practice found that forest bathing also reduces anxiety and depression levels and improves your overall attitude. Besides the emotional and psychological advantages, it has also been shown to help reduce bodily inflammation, improve immune function, and reduce heart rate and blood pressure, among other physical health benefits.

However, in America, there is an inequity problem that often discourages Black and brown folks from seeking access to green spaces. This is true for many reasons. First, there is systemic segregation that confines most Black folks in inner cities and away from expansive land plots and green spaces. As you may know, green spaces—even public sites—aren't always safe or welcoming for Black folks. Such was the case for birder Christian Cooper when a white woman with a dog threatened to have him arrested by police. His so-called crime: He asked the woman to put a leash on her dog, a legal requirement in that area of New York's Central Park. Thankfully, Cooper was not arrested or physically harmed. However, this was a cautionary tale for African Americans—especially Black men. This makes *existing-while-Black-out-in-public* harder to do.

For mental health reasons, Black people should consider regularly accessing green spaces. Black men have a special need to take a break from external and internal pressures. And everyone needs space to just be with themselves rather than thinking, plotting, and strategizing life's next steps. In addition, if the research is any indicator, your physical health will certainly benefit from the time outdoors.

Take Action

Given the complicated nature of *existing-while-Black-in-public*, you may want to do a bit of research on safe green spaces to visit. You could have your first immersion in a small urban park. If you live near—or have access to—more suburban or rural areas, there are often public trails you can use. Also, you could consider doing this with a small group if it makes you feel safer when you venture into an unfamiliar forested area.

While you are out there, touch a tree, look at and smell the nature around you, listen to the sounds of birds, feel the breeze or warmth, and—if it's legal and safe to do so—taste a wild berry. Spend some quiet time in nature and absorb all the health benefits it has to offer.

Create a Vision Board for Your Career

It may be hard to imagine how a *vision board* can help you practice self-care. In fact, vision boards of years past, often thought of as simple arts and crafts projects, have emerged as very helpful tools in the world of career development and counseling. While they can be tools to embrace manifestation (turning an idea into reality)—and there's nothing wrong with that—they also provide a host of other benefits that go beyond creating something that looks nice on your wall.

When it comes to being a Black man, particularly in America, there is an incredible amount of pressure to be successful. This pressure is not just for yourself and your immediate family, but for many of us, there is also a cultural responsibility to succeed and be a credit to our people. Mostly this pressure is unifying and helpful. However, it can also be completely overwhelming when you haven't decided on a goal or if you're not sure how to go about reaching your aim. A vision board can give you a place to start and to visually chart your path to your desired future.

For Black folks, radical hope is not only a useful tool but a psychosocial necessity in facing barriers to achieving your goals, such as institutional racism and classism. Imagining a world beyond what you see right now, both for yourself personally and for the community at large, is necessary to keep you functional and striving toward a more enjoyable life that is also more sustainable for you and your family.

Vision boards help you unlock your potential. They invite you to use your imagination. They cultivate hope and put you in a future-oriented mindset. This mindset can enable you to move from a stuck position and take steps to create the life you want. Vision boards also help you clearly define the "why" behind all the hard work you will undertake to achieve your goal. And when you feel optimistic about your career goals, it actually leads to an increased chance of success in your career.

Take Action

Today's vision board doesn't have to include magazine cutouts and hot glue as it did in years past. You can create a digital board using a variety of online tools, or simply put together a folder where you collect images and words that inspire you and help you reach your career goal. You might include something that reflects the kind of work you want to be doing, how much money you'd like to make, and anything that indicates the kind of lifestyle you will have when you reach your goal.

This is the place to imagine and explore. Once you have a digital or hard-copy vision board assembled, you can make it more concrete and create SMART goals. But, for now, permit yourself to visualize the future you want.

Conceptualize a Feeling

Many people cannot obtain self-care because they are in denial and avoiding their feelings. And while distractions can be one part of a healthy coping routine, to move toward full integration and healing, Black men have to become intimate with their deeper, inner selves.

If you've struggled throughout some periods in your life, you likely know how helpful it can be to just zone out and escape the pain. Watching TV, playing sports, and having lots of sex (among any other activities) can often serve as a means of distraction and emotional avoidance. None of those things is bad in itself. However, considering how easily such things can prevent you from connecting to yourself, they can be detrimental. When routinely paired with a subconscious desire to avoid deeper feelings, pleasurable distractions can easily turn into liabilities and interfere with daily functioning because the desire for these activities can prevent you from addressing personal pain. Many men find themselves in this kind of cycle because they are unable to name— to label—their internal experiences and feelings.

A simple strategy can be a great place to start. In my practice, I have had Black male clients envision and describe a feeling as a physical object. This process can enable you to transform something vague into something you can better conceptualize. This kind of imagining can help the feelings make more sense even if you don't have the perfect vocabulary to relate how you're feeling.

Take Action

If you often have trouble understanding yourself, this exercise can help provide clarity so you can be better prepared for the next step of communicating your feelings to someone else. To practice this, imagine you're in a blank room—one comparable to the white room from the film *The Matrix*, for example. Imagine you're there alone with a feeling represented as a physical object. Think about how big or small the object is. Does it take up the entire room, or can you hold it in your hands? Consider its weight. Is it heavy or does it almost float away like a feather? Reflect on its color and texture. Is it smooth or rough? Is it like silk or sandpaper?

As you do this, engage in pulling symbols and meaning from your subconscious self. How you experience this feeling and how you now see and describe it is unique to you. Revisit this practice anytime you have difficulty understanding your feelings. Try naming and envisioning emotions as objects until you have consistent symbols that reference each emotion. Eventually, as you start to feel things, these images you've constructed will pop into your mind automatically, offering you the emotional clarity you've been looking for.

Take a Mental Health Day from Work

Career and work take up a lot of time and energy in the lives of Black men. Work is a place where many find great purpose and meaning, yet it can be taxing on our bodies and spirits. Sometimes we need to take a break.

"You have to work twice as hard to get half as far" is a cultural saying that's passed down by generations of Black folks. And while the saying is true, it still underestimates the amount of work Black people must do, or how great Black people have to be, to get recognized and fairly compensated for labor. Most Black folks have internalized this idea to some extent. We observe this reality when white peers are consistently promoted at higher rates. This discrimination is also reflected in the large unemployment gap between Black people and white people. When we have a job, our feedback and ideas can commonly be minimized.

As a result, Black men experience a tremendous amount of unnecessary stress providing for themselves and their families. And while you can seek to change your role, or look for another job, our racialized system of capitalism can be a barrier. All of this pushback reinforces the idea that you need to work harder to be taken seriously no matter where you go. It's a particularly heavy burden for Black men.

As such, it's important to be more intentional about taking days off and more mindful of the need to psychologically detach from work. That means not thinking about work, putting your phone into a message-only mode, or turning the phone off. That also means taking time away from your email inbox when you're not "on the clock." In addition, it means creating a relatively firm routine in which your time off looks and feels drastically different from working.

By disconnecting from work, you can more easily shift to a more positive mood and engage in activities that give you satisfaction. While there is still so much to be learned from workplace wellness research, we do know that having dedicated time off—even in high-stress times—can greatly improve mood and mental health. Studies suggest that detaching from work may even help you avoid burnout and return to work as a more productive contributor.

There is also an access problem as it relates to paid time off work. Some people have jobs that don't provide time off—African Americans in disproportionate numbers among them. Others have time off in their employment agreements but do not request it because they fear retribution from managers, which is a significant disincentive. In other cases, many hourly workers cannot afford to take time off. Regardless of your situation, try to be intentional about how you use your days off. Even during a typical weekend, you can reduce stress and place yourself in a positive mood if you detach yourself from work during those two-day periods.

Take Action

Take a day off. Make it enjoyable. Get some extra rest and do something that feels restorative to you. Everyone needs rest. Your brain and body need time to recover from the demands and stresses of your job, whether you're a laborer who works with your hands or a researcher who analyzes tons of data in a science lab. This is your opportunity and your permission to try your hardest to disconnect from work—even for just a day. Your mental health depends on it.

Express What You're Feeling

It's a common trope that women are more emotional than men, but that simply isn't true. The real difference: Women often have more-developed communications skills and the ability to express their emotions better than men. Emotional expression has been particularly difficult for Black men through history. That needs to change for the sake of our mental health.

There are likely a lot of reasons for this gender-based disparity, some of which have been explored in other activities of this book. But being able to explicitly lay out how you feel and why you feel that way is an essential emotional intelligence skill. Tropes about gender differences in communication greatly overemphasize biology, which indicates we're actually not all that different. The fact is we undervalue the role of nurture in expression and emotional intelligence.

Many girls get reinforcement for using emotional language early in their lives. This behavior gets reinforced repeatedly over time, strengthening a central skill and facet of many girls' upbringing. Mothers, other caregivers, and teachers also tend to spend a lot of time in conversation with girls. High verbal skills get reinforced in many areas of life for girls.

By contrast, Black boys usually can't say the same. Many Black boys, and boys in general, are rewarded for highly physical play that's action oriented and visible. This isn't a bad thing in and of itself; however, it comes at the expense of verbal expression and emotional development. Black boys aren't taught skills to forge relationships. They are then forced to learn later—a frustration for potential partners. Furthermore, they may not learn the importance of emotional language and sharing. It's why so many men are drawn into concepts like nihilism and stoicism. It reflects a paradigm that is intimately familiar and doesn't push us outside of an established comfort zone.

This challenges relationships and relationship development. To deepen relationships and feel more connected and less isolated, good verbal disclosure is necessary. It's difficult to feel close to people when you know little about their inner thoughts and feelings, let alone commit yourself to care for them in any way beyond the superficial. Learning to express your feelings is a self-care strategy because no one thrives in isolation. This is an essential relationship skill that will serve you throughout your life. When it comes to happiness and success in life, emotional intelligence can matter as much as IQ. By boosting your emotional intelligence, you will be more capable of building stronger relationships.

Take Action

Is sharing your feelings emotionally difficult? Do you struggle when searching for the right words? If so, the good news is that it gets easier with practice, and that means you'll become a better communicator.

The first step: You have to generate the courage to take a few risks in conversations. Usually, the best way to do this is to simply start with using "I" statements. For example, when you say, "I feel frustrated," you're letting someone know how you're feeling. That's helpful because it enables anyone who cares about you to respond and be of help. As they say, "Closed mouths don't get fed." If you believe the people around you aren't meeting your needs, try to incorporate more "I feel" statements in your conversations and see how things change over time, both in your relationships and in your own ability to communicate.

Spend Time with a Pet

Dogs are known as man's best friend for a reason. Animals, especially domesticated pets, provide us with some unexpected health benefits. However, some Black men must overcome a historic fear to get those benefits.

The relationship between African Americans and dogs is more complicated because dogs were trained to track and attack Black people, particularly Black men, during slavery and Jim Crow. This point is made in a 2021 article on a website called *Bark* by Joshunda Sanders, who notes that dogs were also misused during the civil rights movement. "The popular-culture connection between Black people and dogs is long and violent, punctuated by indelible images of police dogs (usually German Shepherds) lunging, teeth bared, or attacking civil rights protesters," Sanders said.

We have to overcome this history to experience the joy of animal companionship. Pets offer the companionship and unconditional love you need after a long day or a difficult situation. There is also social science research that shows us that spending time with animals can help us be healthier too.

Dogs can also help you be more mindful. That means paying attention to what your five senses are telling you about the experience you're having right now. Mindfulness has been shown to decrease stress and promote relaxation. This kind of present-centered living is exactly what pets do so well. They are singularly focused on the present. During our interactions with them, we get into the same sort of flow state. It's hard to feel stressed and anxious when you're playing with a puppy. Pets also seem to have a special kind of emotional intelligence that enables them to go directly to people in need of attention. It's not at all unheard-of for a dog to go sit in the lap of some stranger who is struggling, even if they haven't voiced their concerns out loud.

Besides helping you stay in the moment, spending time with a pet also offers other health benefits. According to one study by psychologist June McNicholas, children who grow up in a household with pets are less likely to develop certain allergies later in life. And spending time in the same room with a dog has been shown in research to reduce anxiety and lower blood pressure.

Therapy dogs have also been found to help reduce reported pain and fatigue when given access to patients in pain management. A broad field of research called Animal-Assisted Therapy continues to explore the benefits of the human-animal bond. Researchers are also investigating the health impact of human interaction with all kinds of animals such as dogs, cats, rabbits, ferrets, emus, and horses. Simply put, spending time with a pet can help you take care of your mental and physical health.

Take Action

If you don't have a pet yourself, try visiting with a friend or family member who does and spend some time around their pet(s). If pets aren't an option at all, you can regularly visit a local animal sanctuary or reserve for domesticated animals to improve your mental health. Take time to focus on the present moment and observe the animals' behaviors and appearance mindfully. It also might be worth considering volunteering at a shelter or fostering a pet so that you get the benefits of the human-animal interaction even if you're not ready for the permanent commitment of pet ownership yourself.

Reflect On Your Experiences with Anti-Black Racism

Racism is a pervasive and insidious force that impacts virtually all aspects of everyday life for Black people. As a result, it can be difficult to process the impact it has on you.

Healing for Black men starts with recognition that you are not immune from the psychological and emotional impacts of anti-Black racism. It may sound unnecessary to say, but it's not uncommon in my work as a mental health professional to hear Black folks minimize the impact societal racism has on their everyday lives.

There are a couple of general reasons for this. First, let's review the stressors. The sting of racism is ever present for Black people globally, especially in the United States. Not a day goes by that anti-Black sentiment isn't being shared by some politician, public figure, or influencer. Beyond that are also acts of violence against Black people—often Black men—by police. It is a lot to deal with, and it's normal to detach. Because this kind of pain is so ingrained in daily life, you may find it tempting to tune out from time to time. Separating yourself from this racial trauma is a helpful tool. But when overused, this kind of detachment can also rob you of the space to honor the impact fully.

Every Black man has a story. Whether that story is fearing for literal physical safety in a predominantly white environment, facing some undeserved interaction with police, or facing racism in their career, most Black men have way too many stories of abuse, mistreatment, and invalidation. Stoicism is a very popular way to avoid that emotional pain. But where does all that pain go?

Telling your story can be an incredibly helpful tool in healing from anti-Black racism. It also helps you manage the internalization of anti-Black racism and all the difficult feelings that come with it. Storytelling is not only an exercise in self-care but also a critical tool in Black liberation. Reflecting on your story and experiences helps you minimize the lingering impact of that racial trauma on your mind and body. And we all could certainly use less of that taking up space in our spirits.

Take Action

If you're not yet comfortable sharing your anti-Black racism experiences with someone in your life, you can start by writing out an experience like a story. Include the details of your experience and how it made you feel. There's no need to tie up the story in a nice little bow or give it a happy ending. That isn't what this is about. Permit yourself to be honest about your experience and the real impact of racism. If you're up to it, create some space with a friend or ally (or even a therapist) who will listen to your story and help you figure out what next steps make sense for your healing.

Read to Reduce Stress and Anxiety

Reading can be a mind-expanding experience when we explore the stories of people different from us. It can also be an incredibly effective way to reduce stress and anxiety, conditions found disproportionately in the Black male population.

Many adults say they struggle to read with any regularity, citing their work schedules and family obligations. Also, for many, reading is a chore or just another task to tag on to an already long day. In addition, selecting the right book is a challenge for many who don't read regularly. It's even hard to find books that focus on the Black experience, as white authors get a disproportionate amount of coverage in the press and on popular book-centered social media accounts. How did we get so far from the experience of reading for pleasure?

Reading is one way to practice self-care for your mental health.

A study conducted at the University of Sussex found that reading could reduce stress by up to 68 percent. Reading was found to reduce participant heart rate and increase muscle relaxation. In comparison, listening to music reduced the levels by 61 percent, having a cup of tea or coffee lowered them by 54 percent, and taking a walk by 42 percent. Playing video games brought them down by 21 percent from their highest level but still left the volunteers with heart rates above their starting point.

And what's even more special about this study is that it didn't even take participants a long time to get this positive impact. The study found that it only took *six minutes* for people to experience relief. Perhaps practicing self-care doesn't have to be as complicated as we tend to make it.

One important point to consider here is that while the type of book or reading material doesn't really matter all that much, you should generally opt for something you think you would enjoy. While you may want to educate yourself on some important topic or historical knowledge, the contents of those books might also increase your physiological level of stress. Reading the news online is almost certain to have the same kind of negative impact.

Be conscious of what you choose, but don't overthink it either. The purpose of this reading is to give yourself and your mind a little time out from whatever else is going on in your life or day. Take advantage of it, even if only for six minutes.

Take Action

Head to your local bookstore and browse until you find something that really interests you. Again, this isn't the time to focus on gaining knowledge—unless that relaxes you. This is an opportunity to find and connect with a book mindfully. Create some time (at least six minutes per day) to enjoy reading the book you chose. After you wrap up each reading session, take a moment to take stock of how you're feeling. Are you feeling more relaxed?

Change Your Perspective

Have you ever found yourself stuck in the same old places, looking at the same old things time and time again? If so, it might be time to change your perspective.

Finding new ways to think about things, shifting your perspective, can be incredibly liberating. Have you ever been driving in a car along a familiar route, and before you knew it, you found yourself at your destination but couldn't recall what the drive there was like? This is because the road is so familiar to you that you've become habituated. Unless you see something new or experience something in a new way, the all-too-familiar course simply fades into the background. If you've ever experienced this, you may have felt a little scared or unnerved when you arrived at your destination. The good news is that more than likely, you didn't "black out." Instead, your brain essentially took a shortcut and processed all those travel details and choices as background noise, giving it the space to focus on something else.

Being able to automatically process extraneous data from your environment is a gift. It allows you to focus your attention and time on something else—often something that requires more brain power. The downside of this is it makes it hard for you to meaningfully engage with an environment familiar to you because you've likely committed all of it to memory. You have to be more mindful and intentional to change your perspective.

Mindfulness—being aware and being in the moment—has been found to reduce stress and anxiety and promote relaxation. One common way people approach mindfulness is by meditation or mindful breathing, but you can also do anything mindfully, from walking to taking pictures with your smartphone.

Take Action

If you want to easily experience what it's like to change your perspective, then consider going to a place in your local area you're familiar with. The place could be outside or indoors, but it probably shouldn't be somewhere that you visit every day. Ideally, you want to visit a place that's familiar, but not too familiar.

Take out your smartphone, or a camera if you happen to have one, and take on the role of an amateur photographer. Take your time and zoom in on certain sections of the place, get low and capture the scene from a different height, or stand up on something and snap away.

Once you're done, take some time to reflect on how the experience felt. Did you feel more stressed or at ease? Did you see anything that you haven't seen before or appreciate something in a new way? If so, you've probably gained some perspective on the benefit of slowing down and taking a fresh look. Think about how you might apply this lesson to other areas of your life too.

Lean Into the Power of Collective Healing

Many communities of color have a foundation of collectivism, which is a focus on the importance of the family and community. While this can have its challenges, especially as it relates to finding ways to prioritize your self-care, existing within the community can also be profoundly restorative and healing.

As a result of colonization, the globalization of ego-centered thinking, and the more recent advent of social media, it is easier than ever to get caught up in a belief system that life starts and ends with you. This growing culture of narcissism and "main character" energy continues to pull us all from one universal truth: None of us makes it through this life alone.

Maybe you've been experiencing a deep sense of loneliness and isolation. Many people who struggle with mental health issues do. It can be isolating to think that no one understands you or your experiences.

Black men face unique challenges in fostering community due to long-standing stereotypes of the "cool" Black man who doesn't need the same support and care that everyone else does. Feeling like you're out on an island alone, especially if you've felt this way before, can make it difficult to move out of a mindset that no one wants to support you. It can be easy to believe no one wants a meaningful connection with you.

Existing *in-community* gives you space to thrive and embrace radical healing. Being in spaces with other Black men enables you to embrace the kind of authenticity that other environments discourage or identify as harmful, unprofessional, or inappropriate. Sharing your personal stories with people who have walked down some of the same paths as you have enables you to build solidarity and gain access to a level of support that might not otherwise be available in your daily life. If you are not currently part of an environment that affords you this kind of space, it may be time to consider finding one.

Take Action

You can exist *in-community* in a lot of different ways. Spending extra time at the barbershop can help you connect with your community. Or you can find communal healing by joining a fraternity or social civic group that focuses on the experience of Black manhood. You may even consider joining a therapy group for Black men. The choice is yours. Permit yourself to step outside of your comfort zone and get to know some new people. Chances are they may be looking for exactly the kind of support you're looking for too.

Visit with Your Ancestors

One of the best ways that Black men can practice self-care that liberates is to embrace connections with their ancestors. Much of how we understand Blackness is framed by elements of the dominant culture— among them, Christianity, colonization, racism, and oppression. Healing for Black men is about embracing the power of self-definition and cultural authenticity by broadening the scope of stories and perspectives on Blackness as an identity. Ancestors, and their spirits, can be our teachers.

The concept of connecting with your ancestors may not be a new idea to you, but it can be difficult to imagine how to go about developing a meaningful relationship with elders who are no longer living or ancestors you've never met. To do this, it's important to connect to the written and oral histories of Black people as a path toward self-knowledge and liberation.

What do you know about the history of your ancestors and their ideas of resilience and fulfillment? If you live in America, probably not much, especially if you've mostly relied on the public education system for this kind of information. Most often, curriculum about Black folks is relegated to Black History Month and a few stories about America's favorite Black heroes such as the Reverend Dr. Martin Luther King Jr. and Rosa Parks. The knowledge gap between older and younger generations is now expanding.

Cultural knowledge of African Americans, and Black history overall, is suffering due to misguided attacks by bigoted politicians and their mischaracterization of critical race theory and age-appropriate education on honest American history. For example, the state of Florida recently enacted the Stop WOKE Act, which prohibits in-school books and discussions about racism.

You can gather such a broad range of knowledge, both historical and spiritual, by devoting some personal time to broadening your spiritual practices and historical knowledge. In her book, *The Pain We Carry*, author and therapist Natalie Gutiérrez explores how connecting with your ancestors with meditation and reverence can help you engage them as guides on your journey of healing and liberation.

It may take some extra personal effort and time to find the ways that are most helpful for you to connect. Some people access this through meditation, prayer, gaining knowledge, or some combination of those strategies.

You also have access to the stories of living ancestors. Black ancestors are in your local community. You can learn a lot about healing practices, spiritual guidance, and the power of family and community from folks who grew up and matured during different periods. Let them be practical and spiritual guides for you on your journey. Look to West African civilizations such as the empires of Mali, Ghana, and Songhai for rich stories of pre-colonial cultivation, strength, and resilience.

Take Action

In your next meditation or prayer practice, try to invoke the spirit of your ancestors and be with them. Consider what other steps you may need to take to connect and visit with them more often. The stories of the ancestors and their rituals toward wholeness and resilience are the blueprint to your success and thriving. If you're affiliated with a school or educational institution, research literature about pre-colonial Africa. Visit your local library and access archives about the lives of historical cultural traditions and celebrations. Consider visiting a local bookstore and reading memoirs by leaders in contemporary Africa for more knowledge and connection.

Practice Radical Hope

If you've been paying attention to the sociopolitical environment over the past few years, you likely know better than anyone how difficult it is to feel hopeful when there's still so much progress to be made. For Black men, radical hope can be a self-help asset in the face of ongoing oppression and disenfranchisement.

First, it's important to dispel the myth that to be hopeful you need to be disconnected from reality. You don't have to forgo reality to believe in the power of hope. One way to think about hope is that it's the consideration that there is something beyond your present experiences and knowledge. What if there could be something better on the other side of these challenges?

Psychological theorists have described hope as a process that is both emotional and intellectual. On one hand, hope represents seeking to feel something different from your current experience. On the other hand, it can also represent a belief system or a series of thoughts that imagines how you can achieve a desired outcome. No matter how you see hope manifesting, you usually need an exchange of energy to find hope and inspiration. If left to our own devices, it's natural to get mired in the difficulties and perceived inevitabilities rather than grasp the power of possibility. This is especially challenging for Black folks considering the numerous challenges of everyday living.

You may have already experienced the power of radical hope for healing and liberation. Elders are an incredible source for hope because those who have long memories can detail how progress has been made throughout their lifetimes. They may also be able to tell stories of the changes they saw because of their faith, inspiration from people in their lives, and the heroes of their time.

Within their stories is historical proof of progress. It is the evidence that shows you that your ancestors once dared to hope for a better future and things *did* get better. Progress has been made. While there still may be so much ground to cover in the search for true liberation, there is also proof that radical hope and faith are important facets of any movement that seeks to right major wrongs.

Take Action

How often do you feel hopeful that Black men, and Black folks more broadly, will see true healing and liberation? If that's been a struggle, know you're not alone.

Hope is more than just a wish and a prayer; it is often the foundation for strategic planning and action. Hope is often the driving force of movements that scream, "We deserve better!" You deserve better. Embrace possibility and allow yourself to imagine what could lie ahead in the fight for equality. What could that look like? What would you like that to look like before your soul leaves this earth? Write down some hopeful thoughts to help light your path forward.

Connect to Your Inner Child

If you have wondered about possible connections between your childhood experiences and your adult behavior, you are on track to discovering what psychologists call the "inner child." Black men can heal themselves by connecting to childhood memories that may be disturbing or disrupting their adult lives.

Many of the perspectives you have as an adult are derived from childhood. Parents and primary caregivers can provide foundational perspectives on the world and our place in it. We get these perspectives from the lessons they teach, but we also gain understanding by processing what we observe in those environments. For example, the belief that "people never take me seriously" is a negative frame that can be based on childhood experience. While you certainly may have had many examples in your adult life of people not listening to you or honoring your feelings, this belief may also have roots in early childhood experiences when you felt your parents (or primary caregivers) didn't support you holistically. Maybe it wasn't malicious on their part. Parents can fail to meet their children's emotional needs if they are preoccupied with life's other challenges. For Black families in particular, these challenges may often involve parents who do not address the socio-emotional needs of their children because they are in survival mode, focusing on the work required to provide basics like food and shelter. These experiences form the foundational parts of our conscious psychology. Some memories of those experiences can also be buried deeper, in our subconscious, if trauma is involved.

As you continue to grow and mature, this inner child shrinks. As you develop more complicated relationships with others at school and subsequently at work, your views and understanding of the world become broader and deeper. Still, some foundational experiences from childhood can be unconscious drivers of some behaviors in your life—especially if they go unexamined.

Treating your inner child starts with first acknowledging this part of you still exists. If you can imagine that there is a younger version of you tucked away in your psyche, you are a step closer to understanding how to meet your base-level needs more accurately and improve relationships with others.

Take Action

Now that you're a bit more familiar with the inner child as a concept, take some time to reconnect with this part of you. You can do this by recalling any stories or belief systems from your childhood. Do you often think, "It doesn't matter how I feel; I still gotta do what I gotta do" or something similar? If so, think back to the origins of that message. Perhaps self-help in this case may then include validating your emotions more. Another step might involve finding more supportive people to share your thoughts and feelings with. The goal here is to connect with this part of yourself, without judgment, and allow yourself to learn your vulnerabilities so you can take steps toward responding to them.

Embrace the Wise Mind
for Decision-Making

When you're facing an important decision, it can be hard to determine the best choice; as a result, you experience a great deal of stress. In addition to exploring the pros and cons, there is another way that Black men can approach decision-making while also improving their connection with their emotional sides.

First, it's important to understand how people make decisions. Most people tend to approach choices two ways: based on either highly rational thought or highly emotional reasoning. If you're someone who describes yourself as highly emotional, you likely make a lot of decisions based primarily on feeling and intuition. If you're someone who sees yourself as logical and thoughtful, you likely make most decisions based on rational thought. On one side of things, rational decision-making relies on information by analyzing the situation. Emotional reasoning involves making decisions based primarily on feelings as the key sources of data. You can see quickly how relying too heavily on one over the other can cause problems. With emotional reasoning, you're likely to act impulsively and make choices that aren't well thought-out. With hyperrational reasoning, you're likely to not consider how a choice will emotionally and psychologically affect you.

Men, particularly Black men, tend to fit into the latter category. We are brought up to view decision-making as ultimately a rational process. When you're looking to decide on something that has potential consequences for your life, you need to be very smart about your next steps. However, it's also important to be able to take a fuller, more informed view before you reach your decision.

The Wise Mind is a strategy that looks at both sides of the mind (the rational and emotional minds) as equally critical sources of information. It's a skill from a form of therapy called Dialectal Behavioral Therapy (DBT). DBT was created to help people with serious mental health issues navigate emotional tides with more balanced thinking. The Wise Mind is a key skill for anyone trying to make the right choice in a given situation. Through the lens of self-care, Black men can use this skill to lean into the emotional data that is also required to make wise choices. Being "smart" in this case is about more than just doing what makes sense on the surface.

By creating space to make decisions in this way, you practice taking care of yourself by honoring all of your thoughts *and* feelings.

Take Action

Think of a lower-stakes choice that you may be facing right now—for example, something as simple as what you're going to eat for dinner. First, make the argument for the hyperrational mind and what would make the most sense objectively. Weigh factors such as health and budget.

Now, take a moment to think about what you just want to enjoy and what feels like the right choice.

Next, take a step back, look at all of the data, and ask yourself, "How can I honor both of these perspectives with my choice? Where is the balance?" Use this decision-making process anytime you hope to make a wise decision.

Identify and Name White Mediocrity

When it comes to self-care for often-marginalized folks, getting real about racism, privilege, and white mediocrity can be therapeutic.

It's not at all uncommon for Black folks, even Black men, to struggle to manage the ever-looming threat of being "found out" as insufficient in the workplace. For Black men, this often results in increased stress and anxiety and a compulsion to over-perform. This is impostor syndrome, and it stems from white mediocrity.

In many environments, Black men aren't taken seriously unless they are at least twice as talented, smart, or compelling as their white male peers. Without knowing it, Black men and boys internalize this pressure to show up perfectly in all spaces. While this may be necessary to move ahead in your education or career paths, it's not healthy if you think you have to always prove yourself and your worth. It's important to be okay with who you are right here and right now.

One way to combat this is to acknowledge how white mediocrity shows up around you. Have you ever been passed up in the workplace for promotion because an average white peer gets the nod? Or have you ever had a manager who you thought would not be leading your team if not for their white privilege? Is the evaluation process inconsistent? Does your supervisor rarely seek your input? We've all been there.

Of course, in most cases, there is a need to accept this state of affairs in your environment. You have to do what you have to do to succeed. Sometimes that means you will be over-performing. However, one way to practice self-care is to permit yourself to acknowledge the truth of white mediocrity, even if only to yourself.

Too often Black men focus on furthering themselves by pushing extremely hard and believing that every person in leadership or management got there based on their merits and work history. This quickly turns into thinking such as, "I just need to work harder and I'll get there too." Hopefully, you will. However, given the abysmal rate of Black male leadership in large corporations and organizational boards, it is harder than you think. And that's because it's not just about work ethic, intelligence, or ability. It's about white privilege, systemic Black subjugation, and covert institutional racism that favors the status quo.

When white mediocrity is rewarded, that is a definite result of racial bias. Take care of yourself by acknowledging that white privilege exists and that white mediocrity is celebrated in every facet of culture.

Take Action

As you made your way through this activity, were you able to identify white mediocrity in your life? Can you envision a coworker, colleague, or peer who seems to always stay above the fray despite underperforming or doing the bare minimum? Can you recognize when that person is applauded for the way they appear or talk rather than the actual content of their thoughts and work?

Remind yourself that you belong in the spaces that you have access to and those you have yet to see. Acknowledge white mediocrity when you see it, and resist the tendency to rationalize away the losses that racism hands you.

Find Your Safe Space

These days, it seems there is news of violence against Black men every month. The need for safe spaces for Black men is more important than ever.

It's not common for us to call out racism and oppression and openly talk about the impact that it has on us and our lives. This is, in large part, due to the enormity of the issue. Racism is everywhere. It permeates every facet of life. It's not reasonable to create space for every moment of prejudice or violence toward Black folks. If you did so, you simply wouldn't have any time left in the day for anything else. Compartmentalizing, or putting that out of the mind intentionally, is one way to cope with racial violence and other oppressive acts. There's just too much of it to talk about every bit.

In addition to this, it's emotionally and physically draining to always be constantly in "the fight." Nearly every Black person has no choice but to be coerced into sloshing through the perils of injustice, as it's deeply embedded in most systems. The burden is heavy and the impact of all of that is cumulative. There's not anyone more tired than a Black elder who has been fighting against these isms for their entire life. This phenomenon is called "racial battle fatigue," and it affects everyone from professional activists and advocates for Black students to Black workers in all occupations.

Black people need a place to rest to gain relief from the battle. Black men, especially, need this time and space for relief because we're much less likely to acknowledge our pain and the daily wear on our bodies and souls due to the multiple levels of oppression that so many of us face.

There is no shame in recognizing the need to have that time and space. Rather than looking at this idea of a safe space as a liability, look at it as a kind of "waking sleep." Every human being requires sleep. It is restorative. A psychologically safe space is the waking version of the sleep we need. It's the restoration that helps you keep your body stable and healthy and ready to respond to the next day's challenges.

Take Action

If you haven't yet begun to identify a safer space for you, this is a good opportunity to brainstorm on what would be most helpful for you. Instead of seeking out one space, it's important to create a few options for yourself because, at any given time, the space you seek might not be readily available.

Some options to consider are literal physical places like a spot in your home or community, such as a park, barbershop, etc. Or this might involve objects that help you feel grounded, such as a meaningful gift. Or it could involve connecting with loved ones you can rely on. Save your safe space short list in a place where you can find it so that you can easily be reminded of what helps you feel grounded and safe when you need it most.

Make a Positivity Playlist

Music is a powerful force in most of our lives and can be integrated into self-care routines.

If you've ever needed to gas yourself up for a presentation or other kind of performance, you probably know how music can energize and inspire you to rise to the occasion. If you've ever rallied after a long day at work to spend time with friends until late in the evening, you know how much difference a good song can make.

We often turn to music when we're feeling down or sad. At other times we turn to music to be soothing background noise when we're at work or resting. For many people, music is also a part of their exercise routine. But why is that? What purpose does music serve for us in terms of mental and physical health?

Music has a lot of benefits beyond being something that you enjoy. In studies it has been shown to help reduce stress and anxiety. Music can also enable you to cope with difficult life situations. According to the American Music Therapy Association, while figures throughout history have written about the healing power of music, it wasn't until about the 1940s that it started to emerge as a form of therapy. If you've ever had a particularly bad breakup, you can probably point to a song or two that helped lift you out of your deepest, darkest moments. Or maybe you have a song that helps when you're grieving someone you lost too soon.

Music therapy research tells us music helps us process emotions and cope with difficult situations and reduce anxiety. In one University of Pennsylvania study, the song "Weightless" by Macaroni Union reduced anxiety and patient pain during medical procedures; it even had a similar effect to a typically prescribed sedative. Music is powerful!

Music can help improve your mood or send it tumbling down the drain. It depends on your selection and the situation. If you approach music with some intention, it can become a low-lift self-care activity for you.

Take Action

Now is the time to lean into the amateur DJ that lives inside you. Instead of creating a playlist to get the party started, create one that can help you on some hard days or when you're feeling stressed-out and anxious. This is also the time to reflect on what actually makes you feel good rather than focusing on the typical songs that you think are *supposed* to make you feel good.

Perhaps you should consider music from a different genre (or even language). Expose yourself to a range of music and observe how you respond to it. Do you feel more relaxed or upbeat? Do your worries seem to shrink? If so, then you've probably found a good option to add to your playlist. Continue to build this out over time until you have something that can be a reliable tool when you need a little extra help getting back to your usual self.

Develop Your Spiritual Self

Given the lack of attention paid to the mental and emotional lives of Black boys and men, we often struggle when we try to connect to deeper parts of ourselves. Spirituality, and a sense of connectedness beyond what is immediately observable, suffers as a result.

There is a common stereotype that all Black people are religious or spiritual by default. While it is true that many Black folks will identify themselves as such, it's also important to recognize that cultural attitudes and beliefs are shifting as time moves forward. You can decide for yourself whether that's a good or bad thing, as that is beyond the scope of this exercise. The purpose here is to help you reimagine your spiritual self as a tool for self-care.

When scholars talk about resilience and liberation in Black communities, religion comes up often. Spirituality does as well, but given that spirituality is much harder to describe and observe, it's harder to capture the full range of people's beliefs—especially if they fall outside dominant religious doctrines. Also, most of the research within Black communities centers on the spiritual experiences of Black women. Black men and their beliefs and experiences are often left out of the conversation because they don't participate in religious convenings as much as Black women. Some would argue that men in general are less spiritual. But I would argue that spirituality may be playing a bigger role in your life than you think.

Have you ever been in an interaction with someone such as a coworker or colleague and had the impression that they weren't being entirely upfront with you? That was probably your intuition working in the background, which is a function of spirituality. Have you ever traveled to a place away from home and felt "at home" with other Black folks you encountered? These are also spiritual experiences.

One of the functions of spirituality is that it can offer a sense of knowing without having the observable data to back up your theory. And for Black folks in particular, spirituality offers us this feeling of connection to kin—both present, past, and future. That's why we need to invest in our communities; that connection withers and dies without community. As such, nurturing your spirituality can help you practice self-care in two concrete ways: 1) it offers you a sense of knowing and intuition that can help guide your choices and actions, and 2) it provides a never-ending sense of connection and belonging to your community. Whether you invest in developing this part of you in a traditionally religious or a humanist-spiritual sense is up to you. However, the benefits can be incredible for your mental health no matter what form that looks like for you.

Take Action

One way to further develop your spiritual self is to reflect on your personal beliefs and values. For example, how do you find value and meaning in your life? When, and with whom, do you feel most connected and grounded? How do you make meaning out of the good and bad things in your life? Take some time to reflect on questions that will provide further insight on how to continue to build your spiritual work moving forward. Reflect on your personal history with religion and/or spirituality. Consider what may help to revisit now or broaden your research to consider other spiritual practices and traditions that may now meet your needs.

Get a Massage

We Black men hold a lot of tension in our bodies. That is evident when you consider that our population suffers disproportionately from high blood pressure. This is compounded by the fact that we don't have many spaces to speak honestly about our feelings and struggles without fear of being shamed or ridiculed. All of those feelings, thoughts, and stress stay inside. We know that this affects us mentally. But many of us do not know it can also afflict us physically.

Stress, especially when related to prejudice and discrimination, can have serious health consequences. Racial stress contributes to chronic inflammation in the body, which can negatively impact major organs such as the heart and lungs. The relationship between racial stress and an increased risk for heart issues and hypertension is well documented. Therefore, it's important for Black men to be more conscious and intentional about finding self-care practices for the body as well as the mind.

It may surprise you to learn that massage therapy can be a remedy. Most people see a massage as something that just helps them relax. But there are physical benefits such as the reduction of the anxiety and stress that cause physical problems. While this is true, the benefits are more layered and complex than that.

Human touch is a vital part of the human experience. It is something most of us have missed consciously or unconsciously during the physical isolation measures of the COVID-19 crisis. Human touch and actions such as hugging help produce oxytocin, a naturally occurring human hormone that helps people feel bonded and connected. It helps put us emotionally at ease. Also, consider this: It is the same hormone that is readily produced when you pet a dog or when a mother cradles her baby. Even if a pet or baby is not part of your life, you can lean into this therapy by hugging friends and loved ones more and by getting periodic massages.

Moreover, massage therapy has also been shown to improve immune function and help reduce pain related to chronic health conditions such as rheumatoid arthritis and fibromyalgia, especially when received regularly.

If you decide to try this method of self-care, you'll want to get an artful massage, one that reduces bodily tension through careful manipulation of the body's tissues, muscles, and joints. There are a variety of options, but consider the following two choices: the Swedish method—often thought of as the "relaxing" massage—and shiatsu. More traditional massage therapy focuses on the muscles. A shiatsu practitioner focuses on joints and connective tissue.

Take Action

If you've never received a massage before, it can be an uncomfortable experience initially, but don't let that deter you. Do your research by looking up different methods online. Ask friends and relatives if they can recommend a top-notch massage therapist.

Taking those steps can go a long way in helping you feel more comfortable if this is new to you. Also, don't be embarrassed to ask questions. Massage therapists are a wealth of information about what helps the body release tension.

Write Your Own Obituary

For most people, death is a scary concept. No one really wants to spend time reflecting on the end of life and mortality, but doing so can enable you to gain some perspective on your life.

If your life has been touched by grief, it can feel as if the world stopped moving. You can easily get trapped in grief from the shock of losing someone you love. One way to honor that loss is by giving yourself time to reflect on the loved one's life and what it meant to you. You may typically do this in your community, but there are certainly times in which that's an individual pursuit too.

Grieving in this way enables you to reflect in a way that results in "meaning-making," a process that helps you honor your feelings by recalling memories and by exploring the value of that person's role in your life. It's an act of deep love. We don't often engage in that kind of reflection regularly, and that's too bad because it can also enable you to gain perspective as you move toward your own life's goals.

This process of reflection offers you a depth of perspective that's uncommon in daily life. Just think about the last time you read someone's obituary. Sure, the most basic ones may provide a superficial picture of that person's life and what they meant to others. However, others are more detailed and adequately capture the late person's acts of love and connections, and the departed's commitment to that community—the individual's legacy. When it's your time to pass, how would you like to be remembered? Who would you like to be referenced in your obituary? What will your legacy be?

These kinds of questions can help you focus more on the most important things in your life. Allow yourself the space to imagine your ideal legacy, then recalibrate and get back to work on making those dreams come true.

Take Action

Take some time now to craft your hypothetical obituary. As morbid as this may seem, it can provide a lot of perspective on where you are in life, where you ultimately want to be, and the impact that you want to leave on others—*your* legacy.

Let this exercise enable you to reflect on your life and how you want to spend the rest of it. Check back a few months later to determine whether you're actively working toward those goals or not. If necessary, you can regroup.

Clarify Your Personal Values

There is a lot of noise in our current environment. With that comes a lot of opinions and perspectives on how we choose to move throughout life, often without solicitation. It's part of the price we pay for living part of our lives online. Considering that all of us—especially Black men—must create more space to quiet the noise to clarify what we find most important instead of regurgitating messages from what we read and watch from influential creators in our community. Not all skinfolk are kinfolk, and it's important to be discerning with what messages we, as Black men, continue to internalize.

If you spend time on any social media site these days, you've likely realized how difficult it can be to have normal conversations with strangers. This is in large part due to a disinhibition effect that enables you to say something online that you wouldn't necessarily say to someone in person. This has its benefits, especially if you struggle with social anxiety but still want to make connections. Talking online can be easier. One major disadvantage, however, is that it can easily lead to a lot of commentary and feedback that can affect the choices you make. Much of the content online is negative and toxic. It's hard to avoid internalizing this kind of messaging—especially when there is so much of it—unless you keep your values clearly in your mind. For Black men in particular, a lot of popular voices online reinforce limiting Black male stereotypes around infidelity, accumulation of wealth, and the Black alpha male ideal. We can honor our strength without making it our entire personality.

Being mindful of the time spent, as well as the kind of information you're encountering, online is a way to maintain a healthy mental state. It's easy to lose a sense of self when you're routinely flooded with either good or bad commentary on everything you share online. You can practice self-care online by setting boundaries on the topics you discuss and by being mindful of the feelings of others. This is an expression of values—your best self.

Self-care also means taking time to recenter yourself on your values as you divest from the noise of online communication, which can be harsh toward Black men.

If you take time to gain clarity on your values, you can readily identify the steps that are necessary to achieve the life that you want. Also, self-determination is an under-discussed factor in mental health. Being able to decide who you are and what you value most is a way to lean into self-determination. And when you focus on yourself and your deepest values, you practice self-care by investing in a deeper emotional and intellectual life. Without clarity on these values, you can easily wander through life aimlessly, feeling confused, overly focused on the opinion of others, and anxious about what lies ahead of you. While this kind of exploration may not feel good at the start, it can enable you to see the possibility within your future and give you the much-needed motivation to push forward despite whatever challenges lie in your way.

Take Action

What do you think you value the most? What principles do you live your life by? And have you been listening to yourself or the noise from others around you? Take some time right now to focus on these questions. Consider journaling your answers and identifying a few keywords that feel important and deep-seated. Once you have some clarity on what values you most want to embody moving forward, start to plot out specific actions (maybe even revisit the exercise on SMART goals) to help you get closer to becoming the man you want to be.

Address a Mother Wound

Black women are heroes in the Black community. Whether they are single mothers or not, Black mothers represent the connection to both familial love and community. Grandmothers, in particular, are powerful forces often operating as a family's matriarchal leader. However, just as Black men and fathers need to be held accountable for their choices and actions, Black sons also need permission to address the wounds caused at the hands of Black women in their families.

Taking an honest look at the relationship between you and your mother is hard for most people. In my experience as a therapist, it can be difficult to give yourself permission to acknowledge and verbalize how you may have been harmed or disappointed by your mother. It's a special kind of pain that, ironically, is incredibly common.

This is not an indictment on motherhood. It is an incredibly complex experience. In particular, raising Black boys in this day and age is no easy feat. There is room for compassion when it comes to acknowledging the relationship between you and your mother's behavior. However, that also doesn't mean that harmful mistakes by your mother deserve to be minimized or invalidated either.

All mothers struggle to understand their children, and they learn how to differentiate their own needs from that of their children's. They make sacrifices the best they know how to create the kind of life they think their child deserves. They also make mistakes and bad choices that ultimately do not serve their children well at times. For example, a mother may try soothing a Black boy's aching heart by telling him, "You've got to be strong," or otherwise minimizing his experience by not actively listening. In these situations, the best mothers can do is apologize and make amends. Without that acknowledgment, the pain can linger for children.

Many Black men and boys have also suffered trauma from abuse by their mothers. Cultural and societal messaging reinforces the idea that family comes first, and you should "never talk ill about your mother; she's the only one you got." These kinds of statements are painful and retraumatizing for Black men who have lingering pain from experiences with their mothers. Collectively we must do better to honor the pain that Black men have suffered at their mother's hands. Freedom from this pain starts with acknowledging the truth and impact of your experiences.

Take Action

Take some time to reflect on any wounds you may have in your relationship with your mother, no matter how big or small they might be. Allow yourself to grieve the moments you wish had worked out differently. You can also imagine an ideal relationship with your mother that has yet to materialize. You deserve the space to honor this pain without qualification. This process is essential to healing deep relational wounds. Doing so will help you approach relationships with more clarity and meaning.

Limit Your Time on Social Media

When smartphones were introduced to the market, very few of us thought the devices would become virtual, extended parts of our bodies. While we've greatly benefited from this new technology, it can also harm our mental health. It's time to reconsider how we use the Internet and how frequently we use it.

Social media use has increased dramatically in the past 15–20 years. In 2005, just 5 percent of American adults used any social media platform, according to the Pew Research Center. That number jumped to 50 percent in 2012, and now as many as 72 percent of American adults use social media daily. Social media has changed our norms as it relates to the sharing of information, and it has created a new form of community for those who use it frequently.

While there are certainly many benefits of engaging socially online, it also comes with hazards. Black Americans use *Twitter* at a higher percentage than other groups in the country, according to a study by the Pew Research Center. Black Twitter, an Internet community within the *Twitter* network, has been a very popular platform for discussing issues important to African Americans. It is a digital community.

However, spending a lot of time on any social media platform also means you're likely to encounter online trolls, racist comments, and stories and videos of mistreatment and violence directed at both Black men and Black women. You can be exposed to this kind of content in ways you never anticipated. When it comes to Black men, this also means seeing videos and imagery of people like you being mistreated and/or killed by civilian racists and law enforcement. This adds to the growing amount of traumatic stress that Black men experience. Considering the ongoing negative stereotyping and even the belittling of vulnerability shown by Black men, being online can be a not-so-safe space.

More broadly, research has shown that spending a lot of time on social media can lead to mental health problems. For example, a 2018 study of students at the University of Pennsylvania found that decreasing social media usage to just 10–30 minutes per day can increase overall well-being and help limit feelings of depression and loneliness.

One way to take better care of yourself and your mental health is to reduce the amount of time you spend on social media sites. This will help limit exposure to harmful images and impactful material.

Take Action

Now is the perfect opportunity to take stock of your relationship with social media. Do you generally find it to be helpful or harmful to your mental health? If you currently use a smartphone, this might be a good time to assess the amount of time you are on social media apps/sites and see if you can reduce your time. According to 2022 statistics, most Americans spend over a combined two hours daily on social media. If you don't think you can manage to reduce to just thirty minutes daily, create a plan to gradually reduce your time over a longer period and reflect on how the change feels for you. You might be surprised by how good it feels to spend that extra time on something more enjoyable that brings you more peace.

Embrace Racial Pride Through History

When was the last time you truly felt connected to your history?

One of the unfortunate legacies of the enslavement of African peoples in the Americas is the disconnection between Black folks and our African ancestors. One way you can continue to liberate yourself from white supremacist ideals is to connect more deeply to historical knowledge.

In most schools in the United States, there is very little education about African-American history, let alone the history of Black folks globally. Most information is limited to a few well-known Black inventors and activists during Black History Month in February, the shortest month of the year. Sociopolitically, the fight rages on to ensure that younger generations are armed with the knowledge and power of their ancestors—the creators of great West African civilizations, for example—to inspire them to levels of greatness.

For those out there who are no longer in school or higher education institutions, this kind of learning has to be taken up on a personal level. This isn't that easy to do when you have more urgent life matters to tend to than reading about the past. But connecting with the ancestors is about more than learning the facts and stories of history. It's also about learning to embrace ancestral pride.

Developing a meaningful connection to your ancestors helps increase racial pride, which can help further develop a sense of hope. This is particularly important given the political climate and the ongoing battle to put an end to educational censorship that covers up our history.

In addition to developing this sense of hope (which is in and of itself healthy), pride in your heritage also offers inspiration to continue to challenge the current social norms through advocacy and activism. By taking time to learn and honor the stories of your ancestors and Black contemporaries across the globe—their trials and successes—you gain insight and inspiration to continue the battle you're faced with daily.

History helps dismantle common stereotypes and tropes about the Black experience. If you can look beyond the crumbs that the current educational system offers in terms of Black history, you'll learn that Black folks have a range of storied lives, experiences, and healing practices. Being able to have a broader view of Blackness will undoubtedly offer you the space to continue to reimagine and define what it means to be a Black man and develop a sense of pride in your identity and inherited legacy.

Take Action

Learning to appreciate your heritage can be both a solo and a group pursuit. You may want to start to trace your family tree and learn more about your ancestors, either through research and personal family archives and oral histories or through using online-based genetic testing and researching services like African Ancestry. You may also engage in communal learning by exploring stories and cultural artifacts alongside friends or loved ones so that they can also learn about the contributions of Black folks throughout history. This may look like visiting museums dedicated to the Black experience, watching documentaries, and participating in book clubs dedicated to Black history throughout the diaspora. Be creative in your approach if exploring pride in your heritage hasn't been a part of your self-care routine thus far. Find ways to learn and appreciate the beauty of Blackness in ways that are accessible to you.

Heal Through Dance

Dance and rhythmic movement are not just about performance. Culturally, they're also about shifting internal energy and harnessing its power. For men, dance can also be a powerful way to lean into emotional expression and healing. When movement happens collectively—in a club or dancehall, for example—synchronicity creates a specific kind of inexplicable synergy that is often felt but not easily verbalized.

Almost every culture has forms of ritualistic dance. For folks of African descent, dance has a long history of helping mark transitions to new phases of life as well as empowering individual and collective healing.

In recent history, Black Greek Letter Organizations have tapped into this synergy through stepping performances and exhibitions. Step shows are not only a demonstration of talent but also serve as an entertaining way to display brotherhood and sisterhood. These performances take a lot of hard work and dedication as fraternal families collaborate on a shared goal while simultaneously honoring the rich history of stepping. It is often thought that stepping evolved from enslaved people in Africa to facilitate nonverbal communication without the use of singing and drums.

Movement through dance, much like acting, is the physical embodiment of storytelling. It helps connect to deeper emotions without words, creating an experience that is not just understood but felt. Movement rituals become part of a group's collective consciousness much in the way Negro spirituals helped early enslaved Black folks cope in the antebellum United States. That is, the meanings behind those songs, much like ritualistic dances, are deeply understood within Black communities without explicit verbal clarification. This kind of communication is a part of the connection you still have to your ancestors.

Dance therapy and healing through movement have also become part of the aligned therapies in the modern West as well. Dance and movement therapy is a form of art therapy that helps use movement to connect to emotions and process and work toward healing trauma. This form of therapy borrows (or appropriates, depending on its form and delivery) the historical African and indigenous healing rituals mentioned in this activity.

Take Action

Even if you don't think dancing is your thing (and it's okay if it's not), try a dance class to get out of your head and more into your body and your feelings. Try some form of dancing with roots in African practices for a more intentional and spiritually connected experience. Contemporary African dance often blends movement from across the continent and diaspora. Many dance studios offer open-level West African classes (which may include steps from Adzogbo and Lamban, for example) as well as Afro-Caribbean, Brazilian, and capoeira, which also stem from African traditions.

If you're not comfortable moving in that direction, you can also step outside of your comfort zone by attending a dance-based performance such as a step-dance show, contemporary dance performance, or even ballet. As you watch the performers move to the music, try to reflect on what emotions they may be drawing from and what they're trying to communicate to the audience through their movements. Give yourself space to connect to the feelings you have during the performance and let them wash over you. They may help you connect to a part of yourself you have trouble feeling or expressing.

Personalize Your Environment

Environmental psychology is the study of how the world around us impacts our mental health. Everything from air pollution to noise to the inclusion of green space and art all impacts how we feel every day. We can internalize this concept and apply it to our personal spaces for better mental health.

You can go about this in many ways—in your office at work, a space in your home, or your car. You can play around with colors that help you feel either energized or more at peace. You can include sports memorabilia or other artwork that you otherwise find interesting.

One thing that's often overlooked is including personal and family photos. Of course, having personal photos on your desk or in your car isn't going to do the heavy lifting when it comes to maintaining mental health. However, when the days are long and tough, pictures of people you love and who hope for your success can go a long way in giving you a spirit boost when you need it most. Additionally, if you are someone who values his loved ones or family, that visual reminder can help you refocus on what you value most in your life, enabling you to prioritize accordingly. After all, it is easier than ever these days to get caught up with whatever news or online conversation is dominating the headlines. Having these reminders can help you stay focused as you inevitably start to waver in your attention.

On top of that, it's also a way to passively communicate with other people what you find most important in life. In years past, men used to pull out photos from wallets that were entirely too big to sit on to show other people their families. You'd see their faces beam with pride. Now we have social media accounts that provide that kind of communication. But that's generally for the sake of other people's appreciation, which isn't a bad thing, but it isn't necessarily for your benefit.

Whether it's personal photos of loved ones or figurines from your favorite anime or something else entirely, you can easily practice self-care by curating your personal space with adding a little extra dose of something that feels like you.

Take Action

Take stock of your personal environment right now. You might quickly scan the room you're in, or think of another spot in your home or office. What does the environment look like? And more importantly, how does it *feel*? Does it feel as if it supports your mental health and makes your day more enjoyable? If not, consider how you might personalize your space a bit more. Include more things that represent what makes you happy. Include portraits of family, friends, pets, and other loved ones so that you're always visually reminded of the people you love and who support you the most.

Acknowledge Your Weak Points

As the world continues to shift and change, Black men have to develop a different relationship with themselves and their bodies in regard to their weaknesses.

There is a persistent stereotype that all Black men are strong and always feel strong. As we've internalized this message throughout the decades, maybe even centuries, one unintended outcome of this line of thinking is that being strong is some inherent part of being Black. While there is some truth to this, that strength was passed down through generations. Although there may be an inherited strength, Black men also need space to acknowledge and address the concerns and issues we have with our self-confidence to harness that strength. It can be therapeutic, but it can also be especially hard to share those difficulties with other people.

As a result, many Black men are struggling with their self-confidence and self-esteem in silence. It's important to be able to create space to process your deepest insecurities and feelings about yourself without having to perform as confident and self-assured. This is something that more Black men struggle with than you probably think. Even in the space of therapy and other confidential spaces, it can be hard to face how we feel inadequate.

I want to take a moment to normalize that each person has unique challenges when it comes to how they evaluate themselves. No one is perfect and everyone has struggles, and that's okay. For Black men, being able to acknowledge the parts that don't feel so strong can feel threatening to a sense of identity. But this kind of thinking relies on that old stereotype that there's only one way to be a Black man. You are smarter than that. You're entitled to take time to boost the aspects of your self-diagnosed weak points.

The benefit of being able to acknowledge the parts of you that don't feel quite as strong is that it can enable you to treat yourself with compassion. Additionally, you will be able to identify parts of yourself to strengthen. I can't imagine a stronger quality to have. It takes a lot of courage to face yourself and your flaws. As you identify these weaker aspects, you also may realize that you don't have all the tools to make changes alone. Acknowledging this is also difficult, but it enables you to seek out the resources necessary to help you become the man that you want to be. This type of self-care doesn't feel so light or good, but it can be incredibly helpful and validating. It takes a strong man to be honest and authentic with himself.

Take Action

Create a safe space for yourself where you are alone and can concentrate on taking an honest look at the weaknesses in your thinking and behaviors that might need some shifting. As you do this, don't forget to practice self-compassion and acknowledge that everyone has work to do to become the best version of themselves. This is one important step on the journey toward self-actualization.

Cope with Sexual Dysfunction

The relationship between Black men and our bodies is complicated. On one hand, it's one area of a Black man's life that gets praise and adoration for assumed sexuality, and on the other hand, it fails to recognize the full humanity of Black men.

When we talk about African-American men, the conversation frequently relates to the sexualization of the Black male body. The stereotypes and innuendos directed at Black men are so ubiquitous that they are widely accepted as normal in public conversation.

This fixation on Black bodies is one of the lasting reminders of the enslavement of African people in the Americas. While Black bodies have existed in great diversity since the beginning of time, as a result of the Middle Passage and the enduring legacy of slavery, Black bodies almost universally began to be referred to by their strength and ability to endure hardship. These ideas are at the core of a lot of internalized messaging that complicates our relationship with everything from rest to sex.

For Black men, these messages focus on how well-endowed a Black man is and how well he uses what he has. It's reductive. And what happens when that part doesn't perform in a way that you've been socially conditioned to perform? The impact can be devastating.

A huge industry of pharmacology preys on the anxiety of men of all races from a fixation on sexual performance and internalized inadequacy. Sex is one way that many men prioritize self-confidence. Therefore, when performance suffers, so do self-esteem and self-worth.

But you can adjust your thinking about erectile dysfunction. As sexologist Dr. Chris Donaghue discussed in his work, men must identify that a penis is not a dildo. It is one part of a whole human being. Its performance is directly related to the health and anxiety of its owner. To expect these two things to perform similarly all the time is unreasonable. Losing an erection is not a personal failure. This experience is likely connected to a range of medical issues such as diabetes or hypertension. In that case, it's helpful to see a doctor. However, most likely it is a result of the normal psychological experience (termed by Donaghue as "erectile disappointment") that is wrongly categorized as an erectile "dysfunction." The Massachusetts Male Aging Study of 1994 indicates that at age forty and older, between 40–52 percent of men experience erectile dysfunction. More recently, a 2018 study published in the *Journal of Sexual Medicine* estimates that one third of men are affected by erectile dysfunction. You're not broken. *It is not broken.*

Redefine your relationship with your penis and body. Leave the internalization of the historical messaging behind, and liberate your thinking about emotion and psychology to resolve any issues related to your sexual abilities.

Take Action

Remember that when you engage with someone sexually, you are not a sex toy (and neither is your partner, for that matter). You are more than what exists between your legs, and this part of you is connected to a fuller human being with thoughts, feelings, and insecurities. Recognize that erectile disappointment is not something to feel guilt or shame about. It's a normal part of the human experience. Heal by treating yourself with kindness if and when this disappointment happens. If you have experienced erectile disappointment previously, recall that moment now and practice speaking to yourself more affirming, compassionate messages that you deserved to hear in that moment.

Reflect On Your Positive Qualities

Many self-help approaches focus merely on resolving your flaws and shortcomings. However, acknowledging and appreciating your positive qualities is another approach to self-care.

Acknowledging your strengths is an important part of self-care because most people have a really difficult time with a very harsh internal critic. Black men don't talk about this issue enough. These thoughts can be self-deprecating or shameful, leaving you with feelings of inadequacy. Such thinking can be triggered by negative conversations you see online, or this negative self-image can result from difficulties in relationships, especially with women you are close to.

When you are subject to a lot of feedback and criticism, it can be hard to cope. It's natural to become defensive at points, especially when you feel like there's a personal part of you that's being challenged or attacked. At its best, this feedback is not meant to be punitive or harmful (although it can be at times); it more so represents a call to action for Black men to continue to develop and expand their definitions of healthy masculinity (e.g., being more open, empathetic, and communicative).

A defensive mindset can leave you feeling like no one really cares about you or that no one really cares about the internal lives of Black men. At the risk of invalidating this feeling, it's important to acknowledge that this feedback can be an act of love and a desire for more from Black men. The underlying message is that people, especially Black women, want Black men to win. In this case, winning looks like developing deeper emotional intelligence, becoming a better communicator, and actively taking care of your health so you can be around for a long time for your friends and loved ones. Sometimes that requires very direct feedback. Considering that, you should not lose sight of the things you already have going for you. Try not to be discouraged. It's important to take some time to reflect on your positive traits and characteristics as you continue to do the work of growing into a new way of being.

Take Action

Take some time right now to reflect on your positive qualities. This is something you can write about in a notebook or notes app on your smartphone. Write down at least three traits or characteristics that you can see as being positive or helpful about yourself. If you need some help finding those traits, this is also an activity you can share with friends or other male members of your family. Ask them, "What do you think are three positive qualities that I have?" Be honest with yourself and take time to acknowledge all the work you've done thus far on your journey to becoming the man you want to be.

Get Real about Colorism

Colorism—prejudice against people with darker skin and the privilege associated with lighter skin—can be found in Asian and Latino communities, and it is still too common in interactions among Black people. Despite awareness movements against it, colorism remains pervasive in the Black community.

Colorism stems directly from attitudes that justified American chattel slavery and religious imagery of good (white) versus evil (dark or black). Enslaved Africans were often stratified due to their skin tone. Darker-skinned Africans were relegated to hard labor outdoors, whereas lighter-skinned Africans were forced to directly serve white families indoors.

As Americans began to unpack the legacy of colorism, much of the conversation centered on how lighter-skinned Black people have internalized messages about lighter skin and reinforced messaging about the social inferiority of darker-skinned folks. This within-group conflict is also strategic and reinforces the infighting that helps maintain a racist status quo. Many more Black people have come to understand this; yet these internalized messages remain. Campaigns such as "Black is Beautiful" and songs such as James Brown's "Say It Loud: I'm Black and I'm Proud" have helped a great deal—along with many positive media messages around Blackness. On the other hand, considering the pervasiveness of colorism messaging and its deep colonial roots, healing and liberation for Black men require the elimination of colorism.

Black folks with closer perceived proximity to whiteness still maintain many privileges over darker-skinned brothers and sisters. This impacts every facet of life, including sentencing in the legal system. Reports by the United States Sentencing Commission show that darker-skinned defendants get longer, harsher sentences than lighter-skinned people. Much of the contemporary manifestation of colorism hinges on dating and romantic life as well. Despite our best efforts to challenge the internalized racism of colorism, many people still implicitly prefer partners with "whiter" features and curlier (rather than kinkier) hair. This obviously may not be the case for you and your dating history, but such messaging runs particularly deep and manifests how we use language.

For example, if you still refer to someone as "fair skinned," that is colorism in action as it has roots in a value-based judgment that implies a sense of desirability, rather than the more descriptive "light skinned." Colorism frames lighter-skinned people as delicate, soft, and pleasant, while darker people are often thought of as stronger, harder, and more aggressive. While it may be hard to believe, this implicit association runs true for Black folks ourselves, as evidenced in research by the nonprofit organization Project Implicit.

Despite how far you may have already come with addressing internalized colorism, liberation from this ideology is an ongoing process.

Take Action

How far do you think you've gone with addressing internalized bias and colorism? Take some time to honestly reflect on how this way of thinking has impacted not just how you see others but also how you see yourself. Have conversations with people in your life about the messaging that privileges lightness over darkness and challenge yourself to use language that's more affirming of Blackness. You may even want to consider taking an implicit association test (through Project Implicit) to gain a deeper understanding of your perceptions, which may not be readily known to you at this time.

Learn More about Mental Health and Mental Illness

In our culture, we often look at self-care through the eyes of capitalism and consumerism. While buying things and having experiences that feel good for you are important, sometimes self-care is about arming yourself with more knowledge. For Black men, in particular, this can mean learning more about mental health and mental illness.

If you asked any Black person on the street if their life has been touched by mental illness, the answer would probably be "no." As a mental health professional, I can tell you that's likely not the truth. Our social and educational systems are largely to blame for this. We don't talk about mental health and mental illness in schools. Instead, most often, any conversation around mental health tends to focus on stress management and, at best, emotional intelligence. This is all very helpful, but it leaves members of many communities with a superficial understanding of the complex dynamics and personal issues that you may see play out in your everyday life with friends, family, and others in your community.

For example, substance abuse is a mental health issue. Substance abuse disorders are listed in the current (fifth) edition of the *Diagnostic and Statistical Manual of Mental Disorders*. This is the book that most mental health providers use to help them diagnose and categorize mental health issues. I became aware of this book during my first psychology course in high school. Just as you may have, I witnessed people in my community struggling with substance abuse during my youth. I saw how the community often treated them with either pity, confusion, or contempt, depending on the day of the week. Maybe you've struggled with substance abuse issues yourself or have lived with a loved one who has battled addiction.

Mental illness is not limited to substance abuse issues. Anxiety and depressive disorders are among some of the most commonly diagnosed (and conversely, underdiagnosed in Black communities because there is inadequate access to resources and information). While attitudes are changing about mental health in the Black community, education on these topics must be more normalized. Educating yourself in this area enables you to better recognize symptoms and causes of concern in yourself and others. After all, how can you begin to address what is disrupting your life if you can't even name or describe it to yourself, let alone to others?

Take Action

Many books and articles are available on mental health and mental illness. Some of them are specific to Black and brown communities. To ensure you're getting valid information, look for material written by licensed mental health professionals or professional researchers at your local library or independent bookstore. You can also start therapy yourself. Or you could attend workshops and presentations—in person or virtually—about mental health and warning signs of mental illness at workshops at your workplace or in your community.

When you know better, you do better. Having this knowledge will enable you to respond quickly and more effectively to yourself and people you encounter.

Ask for Help

Previous exercises in this book have taken a look at the trope of the "strong Black man." The refusal to ask for help is one of the most common ways this shows up for many Black men.

Male reluctance to ask for help is a common stereotype. You see it all the time in TV shows and movies. One common scene involves a man and his partner getting lost while driving. The man driving is sure he knows where he's going. The partner is less convinced and wants to ask for help. The driver refuses. It's actually a helpful visible representation of how stubborn we can be when the only thing at stake is our egos.

Most modern Black men don't want to be this kind of unsympathetic character. But more often than not, you may find yourself automatically playing this role. While much of the conversation around this dynamic tends to name the biology of manhood as the culprit, I argue it's largely a result of cultural conditioning.

If you take a step back and think about your childhood, how often were you encouraged to ask for help? How often were you rewarded with support and encouragement once you did that? Many Black men can remember being told when they were younger, especially around homework, to ask for help. But, when that happened, did you get the help that you needed?

As most Black boys grow older, hyperindependence is often a highly valued trait. "You should ask for help" often turns into "You just need to figure it out yourself." Every child needs to learn independence, but when it comes to Black boys (and men), there seems to be a belief that self-reliance is the only way to live. Boys and men often get called weak, dumb, or insecure if they do reach out when they need help. As a result, "Just ask for help" becomes another reminder of how you're somehow failing as a man. This very clearly creates a dynamic in which Black men learn that the only person they can rely on is themselves. This leaves too many men in places where they suffer alone with their problems.

But it doesn't have to be that way! Pushing yourself through the discomfort, and maybe even the past trauma, of being shamed for asking for help can enable you to heal and liberate yourself. It takes a lot of courage to ask for help.

Take Action

You know that you've been resisting the urge to ask for help. This is your opportunity to take that next step and ask for help. No matter how big or small it is, try to push through the discomfort, and maybe even shame, of needing to rely on someone else to get you through. We all need help in life. You can be a strong man and still need help navigating challenges in life. Reach out to trusted loved ones and let them know what's going on. Ask if they have any suggestions on how you can move forward. It may feel scary at first, but after that comes relief. You deserve to feel, even for just a moment, the weightlessness of unburdening.

Embody Radical Acceptance

Living as a Black man in the world today means facing an immeasurable number of challenges, most of which no person should have to face. To cope with what seems like an ever-growing number of difficulties, we disconnect and isolate ourselves. Unfortunately, this leads to internal explosions of anger, sadness, frustration, and trauma. There is another path toward coping, and that path centers on radical acceptance.

Radical acceptance should not be confused with resignation. Accepting your current state of affairs is not just lying down and rolling over. Acceptance is not "giving up." It is recognizing the reality of your current circumstances. This is a powerful act of self-care because Black men are socially conditioned to minimize pain. This messaging creates an ongoing disconnection between your body and mind, creating internal conflict. You can only change this by permitting yourself to honor your experience and all feeling that comes with it.

One reason radical acceptance is so difficult is that it also means acknowledging deep pain. There is so much hurt and harm that take place in our world today. This fosters anxiety and fear within us. Dealing with such complexities and the trauma of racism and oppression causes so much internal tension for Black men. It doesn't feel good or helpful to sit in the pain while you're experiencing it. That's why many people work so hard to stay busy or distracted—it helps you avoid the pain.

But if you're busy avoiding pain, you're also avoiding healing and potential resolution. There can be no solution if you don't identify the problem. What might you be holding onto internally that still requires healing—but you're too afraid to give it the space that it needs?

It's not at all uncommon for people to fear being consumed by their pain. The existential crisis of facing possible destruction or implosion at the hands of trauma and pain is a common fear, even if it's not always articulated in that way. That fear is natural. Pain can be disruptive. But you can take your time and work to accept things bit by bit. And, if you need some help making your way through your hurt and pain, healers and mental health professionals can help guide and support you with radical acceptance.

Avoidance and denial are internal tools we use to help us cope with the complexities of life. There's no need to judge this part of yourself. However, it's also important to recognize that unless you identify the hurt, there can be no healing. Don't allow fear to hold you back. You deserve inner peace as much as anyone else.

Take Action

Take a moment right now to allow yourself to acknowledge some pain that you've been carrying. Try to accept the impact and disruption that it's had on your life. You may want to cry or scream, and if that's helpful, please do so. Take your time. And when you've given this pain some space, you can start to reimagine a new future for yourself while recognizing that some part of this pain may linger.

Explore Music Therapy

Hip-hop and rap—used interchangeably in this activity—are powerful Black art forms. As such, they offer us a safe space to explore language and our experiences in ways that mainstream culture might not always appreciate or value. However, we need to examine the impact rap has on us as individuals and the culture as a whole.

Popularized in the 1980s, rap and hip-hop emerged as a Black music revolution. Following the civil rights movement and Black pride era before it, rap offered a new way for Black folks, particularly Black men, to express themselves. Much of it did and still does reflect on the pain, beauty, and resilience of the Black community. On the other hand, it also monetizes violence and reinforces harmful thinking about women, Queer folks, etc. Rap and hip-hop are as complicated as the people who created them. Therefore, it deserves reverence and grace.

However, there is an opportunity to continue to explore important themes and beliefs critically. Of course, there are times when you need to just enjoy hip-hop for what it is, and there is space for that. On the other hand, if you're more selective, hip-hop can help you continue to grow, and it can be much more personal than just party anthems. As a practice, music therapy uses music as a path to personal exploration and meaning-making. You can analyze the lyrics and mood of a song to reflect on how it impacts you. You can also use it to find in your mind what you need to feel strong and grounded moving forward. Sometimes this involves creating music. Regardless of your method, intentionally choosing to bring some consciousness to your listening or performance experience might be an easier way for you to tap into yourself, learn more, and identify areas for growth.

Take Action

Pick out an album or song that you enjoy and play it aloud as you also read the lyrics. Now, think about your own life right now and consider how the themes or messages in the song apply to you. Are there things you can learn right now? Is there some hurt or pain that the song triggers? What can you do to respond to that pain? Reflect on these questions and see how you can use this information for your growth and self-care.

Foster a Good Relationship with Finances

Building generational wealth is one of the most common financial challenges facing Black people today. It may not seem like self-care, but financial literacy, and gaining knowledge in this area, is vitally important not only for your peace of mind but also for the legacy of your family.

Many Black folks have lacked access to financial information in the past. We have much more access to such information today. In many areas of life, Black people are behind, largely due to the systemic gate-keeping that white folks have employed over generations. Therefore, increasing your financial literacy is a way to create mind-easing security and wealth that can be passed on to family members and your community. When you better understand the economy, the dynamics of finances, and the value of investments, you're able to make sound decisions to better your life and uplift your community.

Black people have a complicated relationship with money and finances. Due to the systemic oppression prevalent in the Americas, many Black people have not had access to the amount of money and resources that people from other racial or ethnic groups have. Additionally, current structures ensure Black folks are regularly disenfranchised and discriminated against in areas that help build wealth—the housing market, for example. You can also see it in the higher interest rates Black people often pay for personal and business loans.

However, strides have been made in limiting abusive and discriminatory lending practices that overwhelmingly disenfranchise People of Color. Black folks have learned more and more about the financial literacy and wealth management required to build more generational wealth within their families and communities. There's still much to be learned, and knowing the basics of financial literacy is a good place to start.

The lust for money stems from the glamorization of extreme wealth and influence, two things African Americans have long struggled to attain collectively. It's important to challenge desires for excess. Yes, you can enjoy the life that wealth provides. However, it is also important to learn financial literacy and money management so your relationship with money is aligned with your personal values. This will help manage any negative impact on your mental health and wellness.

Ultimately, you may want to pass wealth to future generations. If you do more of that, you will also strengthen your community. It is important to navigate the tension between personal wealth and community engagement thoughtfully and holistically.

Take Action

If learning more about financing, budgeting, and investing is something you've put off for some time, now is the time to get started. It can be hard to take an honest look at your finances and debts to figure out where you stand. This often brings up a lot of shame for men, and it's understandable if it brings up myriad feelings or self-critical thoughts. Ultimately, however, looking at your finances more intentionally empowers you with the knowledge of where to get started and what resources you need to reach financial goals for you and your family. Broaden your knowledge by seeking out referrals from friends or business associates for financial advisers, fiduciaries, or certified financial planners they use and trust. You can also speak to your personal banking professionals for more information and do your own research into the many digital tools and apps that help you budget and learn more about investing.

Start an Exercise Routine

Often when we think about health, we only refer to what we call physical health, like blood pressure or weight. We tend to think of mental health as something separate. But the reality is physical health and mental health are intwined. By better understanding the mind-body connection, you can figure out some very straightforward ways to practice self-care.

Movement is essential to your physical health as it offers your body the ability to flex your muscles and joints in ways to help keep you nimble and flexible throughout your life. Movement can also greatly improve your mental health by improving mood, increasing energy, and helping with sleep quality.

Yes, it can do more than just make you feel more physically fit. It can relieve stress and anxiety. With regular exercise, you may begin to experience desensitization to the manifestations of anxiety. For example, people with anxiety often experience a rapid heartbeat and shortness of breath, both of which are very common when you're engaging in strenuous exercise. One reason exercise is so potent in dealing with mental health is that over time you can become desensitized to the body's stress response (which you experience while exercising). As you become desensitized to experiences such as rapid heart rate and shortness of breath, they become easier to cope with when you experience them in settings that generate high stress or anxiety.

For Black men, learning to respond and tolerate exposure to these physiological changes can help promote active coping in the face of ongoing racial trauma, instead of disengagement and withdrawal—which is fairly common in response to racial discrimination in People of Color.

Take Action

If you haven't yet adopted a regular exercise practice, this is your opportunity to start looking for something that fits your lifestyle and health goals. It doesn't have to be complicated. Start in short and small bursts and find something that feels relatively enjoyable to you. After all, exercise is only helpful if it's something you can get yourself to do. And to have that ongoing motivation, it's important to start with something that you might feel excited about. Don't just rely on exploring lifting weights in the gym or running on the treadmill. There are a host of other ways to think about movement. Search for options in your area, which could include things you can do at home. Ultimately, your body will be better for it, and your mental health will benefit as well.

Take Care of Your Sexual Health

As pervasive as sexuality and sensuality are in our culture, sexual health is rarely discussed, and this has serious implications for the lives of Black men.

Did your parents ever have "the talk" with you about sexual health? For many folks, if they did, it focused on the desire to protect young men from getting female partners pregnant. It is with good reason, too, because becoming a parent before you are mentally and financially prepared can drastically change the course of your life. It's important to be mindful of the risks of pregnancy. A lot of sexual activity doesn't risk pregnancy but does still come with the risk of sexually transmitted infections (or STIs). This is something not often talked about within families, and information presented in health classes—if you have comprehensive sex education—is also sparse in most schools.

Many of the stereotypes and perspectives on manhood rely on the trope of the Black man: sexually active, well-endowed, and never satisfied. While it's certainly okay to have pride in your sexual life, you may be surprised to know that these stereotypes have deep roots in how enslaved Black men were racialized and objectified. If you research coverage of Black men publicly during the antebellum South, for example, you'll find details about the brute strength of Black men, often with sexual undertones. Additionally, tropes about the voracious appetite of Black men persisted beyond enslavement in the Americas, which contributed to countless deaths of Black men and boys. Among them was young Emmett Till, who was accused of flirting with a white woman. Neither Till nor his family has found justice.

The internalization of those messages—the hypersexualization of the Black body—continues to put Black men at great risk. Black men should develop the capacity to relate to sexual partners beyond objectification and fetishization, and we can—and should—take necessary precautions to prevent pregnancy and sexually transmitted infections.

Changing the relationship to sexual health is important for Black men's lives on both individual and collective levels. One key way to reduce risk and encourage health-promoting behaviors is significant parental involvement in the adolescent years. This was found to moderate the impacts of peer pressure and risk-taking behavior in a 2015 study published in the *American Journal of Men's Health*. For Black men and boys, liberation from hypersexualization means normalizing risk reduction and regular sexual health screenings as a preventive strategy.

Take Action

When was the last time you had a sexual health screening for sexually transmitted infections? You may be surprised by how many of them can have mild or hidden symptoms not immediately noticeable to you or a partner. If it's been a while, this is your gentle reminder to get a checkup to know where you stand and get the care you need, if necessary. Continue to educate yourself and other men around you about the full spectrum of sexual health and relational concerns.

Become a Critical Consumer of Media

Now, more than ever, we are bombarded with news and advertising no matter where we look. As most of us continue to live our lives regularly connected to our smartphones, it is more important than ever to be conscientious of the media we are taking in. This is especially important in the African-American community because Black people consume more media than other races, according to the Nielsen rating company.

Overconsumption of social media can harm mental health, contributing to anxiety and self-critical thoughts. When you're flooded with the same kind of images and captions daily, it's easy to get lost in the false imagery and expectations that online culture creates.

In addition to the impact of social media, it's also wise to consider to what extent news, entertainment, and advertising influence your behavior. Media of all kinds either includes some marketing or—as is the case with news programming—is surrounded by it in the form of advertisements. Marketing is based on the principles of psychology and behavior change, and it is designed to make money or garner public support. Marketing tactics often involve negative messaging designed to get you to buy a product or believe a certain way of thinking. It is, in part, why fear is often at the core of advertising. "Fear of missing out" and making sure that you're in the company of the cultural elite continue to keep all of us in capitalistic shackles.

One way to take care of yourself and manage the impact on your mental health is to become a more critical consumer of media. When a popular Black celebrity does an endorsement with a global fast-food chain, for example, who do you think benefits most from that campaign? It's not the many Black people who are overweight or obese because they frequently eat this unhealthy food. That doesn't mean that you can't enjoy such things or that you need to shame yourself, but it *does* mean taking a deeper look at the companies that court Black dollars. Are those companies providing community support and advocacy in return?

Modern marketing uses notable people to position them as "authority" figures who consumers are generally inclined to believe. Yet illegitimate authority is often used to influence. You can protect yourself from falling for manipulative advertising by determining whether said authority is legitimate or illegitimate based on their expertise and qualifications.

Take Action

The next time you see a commercial or another kind of advertisement, take a moment to stop and reflect on the message it's conveying and/or the messages it is not presenting. Consider how you feel while being exposed to it and if that might be the intention of the sponsor. How has that message affected your behavior? With this clarity, you can make fully informed decisions about who receives your money or support. Taking the time to consider and evaluate this within the moment can help protect you from undue influence.

Participate and Invest in
Your Community

Self-care is often thought of as an individual pursuit, but it can be so much more than that.

Many men are taught to be self-reliant and hyperindependent. In many ways, this presents a liability that leads to increased stress and anxiety throughout life, particularly as men face systemic issues that cannot be resolved in isolation. The war against prejudice and systemic racism must also be waged within and across communities. To do that, you need to recognize that positive involvement in your community and the communities of other marginalized communities is an effective self-care strategy. When you honor and take care of your community, that same community continues to honor and take care of you.

Engaging and supporting communities helps sustain them and creates opportunities for broader liberation. Practicing self-care in this way might involve attending workshops designed to create ways to heal or improve your neighborhood. You might also participate in wellness fairs and by creating other spaces for more conversations about mental health and self-care.

Intentionally building coalitions with other marginalized communities also helps facilitate global action toward mutually shared ideals such as equality and liberation. One of the key strategies of white supremacy involves pitting oppressed groups against one another so that they do not collectively align and fight the status quo. In short, messaging that puts Black men against Latinos or people who are gay, lesbian, or disabled is designed to prevent all these populations from finding their common ground.

The current systems of thought that question your ability to be a good father, constrain your ability to rise in the ranks because of your skin color, or limit your community's ability to create and sustain intergenerational wealth comprise the same supremacist thinking behind the increased rate of hate crimes against Asian communities during the COVID-19 pandemic. It is the same systemic thinking that threatens the lives of transgender folk. In addition, it is gender biased because the same thinking comes from men who want to eliminate a woman's right to choose. These are different manifestations of the same fight. If you actively participate in your community, you get to take care of and honor yourself as well as uplift other populations involved in the same fight for justice. Liberation is collective.

Take Action

Community care is self-care. Engage in community support and contribute positively to local systems that help sustain your neighborhood and communities of other marginalized people (e.g., women, and disabled, impoverished, and LGBTQIA+ people). You can conduct research to identify community events or problems in your neighborhoods. You can reach out to local politicians and health professionals or gather a few friends together and see what you can do to help communities across demographics.

Prepare a Special Meal for Yourself

Every man needs to be able to cook a meal for himself. It's an essential life skill that some of us learn and apply more than others. Whatever your skill level, learning to cook for yourself is also a way to practice self-care.

Food is a central part of the Black experience. "Soul food" nourishes our bodies and spirits and also connects us to previous generations. Sunday meals are also a way to maintain a connection with elders and less immediate family. Yes, dining out with significant others and friends shows our commitment to spending time with the people we appreciate most in the world. However, good nourishment can also be special when you prepare it at home, and that can be a privilege and a gift considering that—according to reports by the charity Feeding America—fifty million people in America struggle with food insecurity. Many of us have also experienced that insecurity at some point in our lives and now appreciate food with a different kind of gratitude.

Everyone probably knows at least one Black man who really enjoys cooking or baking. It's likely you think of that guy as someone who doesn't fit into the stereotypes that you expect for a Black man. It's fairly well-known that Black communities generally lean toward more conservative and traditional family values. This means we tend to think of the kitchen as a woman's domain, with few exceptions. Today, it's important to collectively reframe cooking as not just women's work but a daily life skill and healthcare practice that every man needs.

To that point, nourishing yourself well (whether you are single or not) is an act of self-care. This means having a diet filled with a variety of delicious and nutrient-dense protein, fruit, and vegetables. It also means that cooking for yourself can be an expression of mindfulness and a practical exercise in self-care. Occasionally moving beyond the quick weeknight meals you might make is a way to lean into cooking as more of an investment into the self, rather than just an essential practice.

Continuing to develop your skills in the kitchen ensures you can nourish yourself by preparing and eating interesting and delicious meals. Just as you can take a mindful walk, you can also prepare meals in the same way. Paying attention to the textures you touch, the process of cooking, the deep scents, and, ultimately, the taste is an exercise in mindful cooking and eating, which can help you improve your physical health. It can also be fun to develop these skills and to challenge yourself with a new recipe with unfamiliar ingredients. And, of course, you get the benefit of the prepared dish at the end too.

Take Action

Even if cooking isn't exactly your thing, try to think of this as an exercise in self-care. You don't have to try out new, complex recipes every time you cook. However, trying something a bit more complex every once in a while requires being present during preparation periods—the same kind of focus recommended in many places in this book. Take the time to sharpen your culinary skills and let daily nourishment be an intentional act of self-care. Get inspired by cooking TV shows or follow tutorials online from chefs on *YouTube* and other social media channels. You can also take a cooking class virtually or in person, solo or with friends, to learn something new.

Release Familial Burdens

Throughout this book, we have explored the multiple ways in which oppression shows up in the lives of Black men and the paths toward healing despite those factors. Another way to move forward in liberation is to release the burdens of your immediate ancestors and your family.

For most of us, exploring intergenerational trauma starts by delving deeply into family history. That includes looking at the history of the Transatlantic Slave Trade and the lives of Africans before slavery and colonization. This kind of exploration helps you embrace deep ethnic and cultural pride. It also helps dismantle some of the internalized racist stereotypes and stories you learn about Black people through a white lens. Intergenerational healing is about examining the plights, stories, and burdens of ancestors within your own family.

Each family has a unique lineage, filled with stories of challenges and triumphs. In almost all families are also tightly held secrets of misdeeds, abuse, and trauma—and this can be especially true for Black families across the diaspora. While no one in the world would want their most difficult family secrets to be publicly laid bare, racism has also reinforced this secret-keeping as Black folks are compelled to work extra hard to minimize and hide any stories that put their families in a negative light. This approach has become so deeply ingrained in Black families that it's also hard to imagine it not being a part of Black culture. It can take years, generations even, for members of families to learn the secrets of their foreparents.

This kind of shame and secrecy also keeps Black men from learning lessons from immediate ancestors and breaking cycles they may not even know exist as those same patterns are normalized within the family. It's often the case that we don't know how abnormal something is until we open up and talk about it with a more objective party. This is something I've certainly witnessed in my work as a therapist.

While it can be difficult to look deeply into troubling family dynamics and secrets, it is an important step in reconnecting with yourself. Doing this work can help you release the burdens and unintended legacies that have likely persisted for generations. This exploration starts with leaving behind the legacy of secrecy and opening up to have meaningful dialogue about family history.

Take Action

Take some time to create a journal on the story of your family and the unintended legacies that persist. Have some topics or histories been ignored or covered up? Are there secrets hiding in your family tree? Are there behaviors or patterns that you've always felt strangely about and don't want to perpetuate? These are all signs that affect how you see and move through the world. Digging deeper and acknowledging them enables you to heal and create a new legacy for your family for generations to come.

Practice and Embrace Joy

What is your relationship to happiness and joy? One of the most underutilized tools in resisting discrimination and oppression is embracing joy. As James Baldwin once famously said, "To be a Negro in this country and to be relatively conscious is to be in a rage almost all the time." I've never heard a truer statement.

There is, of course, plenty to be angry about. Black folks continue to face an incredible wealth gap. Black voter disenfranchisement continues to be a modern problem, despite it theoretically being washed out decades ago. Black women also continue to die at higher rates during pregnancy and delivery due to poor medical care. Moreover, Black men are overdiagnosed for conditions like schizophrenia and don't receive appropriate mental health diagnoses and treatment. In addition, Black people continue to face brutality at the hands of the police. And that's not everything.

It's hard to imagine that all the challenges aren't by-products of the system. Instead, they are part of its essential design. Keeping Black folks in constant loops of trauma and pain wears on our collective and individual psyches. The harm suppresses hope and happiness. And when that harm is everywhere, it can be incredibly difficult to even imagine there is actual joy in our lives.

Black men are also notorious for posing as cool and above it all instead of expressing joy and happiness. This is one of the masks that Black men are taught to put on for the world. However, this is changing thanks to a movement that categorizes *joy* as *resistance*. Kleaver Cruz, a young Black man, is credited with founding The Black Joy Project, a digital and real-world affirmation that Black joy is resistance. This movement has grown to the point that it is recognized in an exhibit at the National Museum of African American History and Culture.

Indeed, joy *is* an act of resistance! Finding peace and happiness when there is tumult all around you is healing. Smiling is self-love in action. Cultivating joy is liberation. These moments are experiences that help you reconnect to all the good things that are still present. When was the last time you leaned into that? When was the last time you genuinely smiled? When was the last time you had fun and felt lighter as a result?

Take Action

For Black men, it can be hard to imagine what joy looks like in your life, especially if it hasn't been an emotion you've felt in recent years. If you don't know where to start, this is a good opportunity to reconnect with your inner child and remember what made him happy and brought him joy. Maybe you need to revisit a game that used to make you smile. Or visit an amusement park if that made you happy as a child. Write lyrics or poetry if you did so many years ago. Go to a dance hall or a concert. Give yourself space to reconnect to whatever has pleased you in this life. Permit yourself to lean into this as not only a part of routine self-care but also an act of resistance. Rage is inevitable. Make joy inevitable too.

Further Reading

I find that reading is as helpful for gaining intellectual knowledge as it is in expanding emotional intelligence. Gaining more insight into what strikes a chord within you and how the environment may be affecting you is critical to understanding your mental health and self-care needs. It cannot be overstated how influential racism, discrimination, and other forms of prejudice influence your thoughts and actions—some of them intergenerational. Along with the strategies and ideas in this book, here are some other books that may help you on your journey of healing and liberation:

All Boys Aren't Blue: A Memoir-Manifesto by George M. Johnson

Personal essays in the exploration of the experiences of George M. Johnson, a prominent journalist and LGBTQIA+ activist.

The Pain We Carry: Healing from Complex PTSD for People of Color by Natalie Gutiérrez

Described as a "powerful guide to unburdening yourself and healing your pain," *The Pain We Carry* is a guidebook on racial healing for People of Color.

We Real Cool: Black Men and Masculinity by bell hooks

In this book, author bell hooks reflects on the difficulties of Black men amid a hostile social environment that dehumanizes Black masculinity. She offers new perspectives on connection and healing.

The Will to Change: Men, Masculinity, and Love by bell hooks

This book changed my life and helped me open up and get closer to my vulnerabilities and emotional life. It's a challenging critique of men and masculinity and a call to action for men to embrace their emotional selves.

Acknowledgments

I never believed I would become a published writer, let alone an author of two books. To say that my life thus far has been surprising would be an understatement. I'm so grateful for the opportunity to provide this book to help Black men take better care of themselves. This book is truly a labor of love born out of self-acceptance and love for my community.

Gratitude is a personal practice of mine, and I'd like to share with you some of the people who helped make this book possible.

To Rebecca: When we first made contact a couple of years ago, I didn't imagine that you'd be my entry point into becoming a real writer—a real author. Thank you for entertaining my anxieties and shepherding me through this process with such ease and grace. I appreciate you!

To the entire Adams Media and Simon & Schuster team: Thank you. The readers may not know, but the publishing process is so complicated! I'm so thankful to each member of the team who said "yes" to my ideas and helped bring them to publication. It's incredibly reassuring that behind each book is a talented team of people who want an author to be successful. I appreciate your hard work and the talent in all you do.

To my business partner and friend, Rachel: I'm thankful to have you as inspiration for living a life with meaning and passion. Thank you for always doing that and for helping to create the space that allows me to be me—whether I'm writing or not.

To my family and to friends who are like family—there isn't much distinguishing between the two for me and you all likely know that by now: Without naming every single person I've been fortunate enough to call a friend over my years on earth thus far, I want you to know that you helped make me who I am and for that I am forever grateful. Whether we are now in touch often or much less than we were before, just know there is a part of me that always walks with you and you with me.

To my mother especially: Thank you for giving me the space to live, work, and create in the ways that are best aligned for me. I know the distance isn't easy.

To my Alpha Phi Alpha brothers, especially Carnell and my LBs, Gorilla Warfare: You probably don't know how much you've taught me about Black manhood. As a Black biracial boy with a Puerto Rican father, you all helped me define and carve out Black masculinity for myself. I appreciate your acceptance and I love you. *Thank you.*

And finally, to every person reading this book: I am grateful to you! Thank you for being vulnerable enough to open these pages and explore what self-care can look like for you. I wish you all inner peace and ease in your life. Take the ideas in this book and continue to build on what self-care needs to look like *for you.* Continue to share what you learn and inspire others to do the same. Thank you for being you and for showing up.

Index

Acceptance, 11, 193–94
Affirmations, 187–88
African-American Vernacular English (AAVE), 41
African Diaspora, 15, 75, 176, 178, 209
Alcoholics Anonymous, 96
Alcohol, limiting, 105–6
Alcohol Use Disorder, 105
All Boys Aren't Blue: A Memoir-Manifesto, 214
Amends, making, 95–96, 171–72
Ancestors
  communication and, 77–78
  connecting to, 149–50, 177–78, 209–10
  fortitude of, 63–64
  racial pride and, 175–76
  resilience of, 63–64, 114, 149–50
  slavery and, 16, 33–34, 59–60, 71–74, 77–78, 111–12, 175–78, 187–88, 209–10
  as spiritual guides, 149–50
Anger, handling, 57–58, 60, 70, 193
Animal-Assisted Therapy, 140
Anti-Black racism, 124, 141–42
Anxieties, 87–88, 129–30, 139–44, 161–62, 199–200. *See also* Stress; Trauma
Apologies, 95–96, 171–72
Arbery, Ahmaud, 53
Art, creating, 71–72, 178–79
Assertiveness, 35, 49–50, 77–78, 99–100
Audio journaling, 41–42. *See also* Journaling

Balance, finding, 11, 88, 97, 104, 156
Baldwin, James, 57, 211
Bark, 139
Bedtime routine, 83–84, 87–88
Black History Month, 149, 175

"Black Is Beautiful," 187
Black Joy Project, 211–12
Black Lives Matter, 76–77
Blackness
  affirmations for, 187–88
  defining, 15–16, 63–64, 149–50, 175–76
  loving, 75–76
  perspectives on, 149–50, 175–76
  understanding, 63–64, 149–50, 175–76
Body
  exercise for, 11, 23–24, 39–40, 177–78, 199–200
  listening to, 37–38
  nourishing, 11–12, 29–30, 33–34, 207–8
  relationship with, 37–38, 71–72, 181–84, 201–2
Books, reading, 89–90, 143–44
Boundaries, setting, 49, 103–5, 170
Breathing techniques, 21–22, 38, 87, 101
"Bro" responses, 49–50
Brown, James, 187
Burdens, releasing, 49–54, 95–96, 135–36, 159–60, 191–92, 209–10
Burnout, preventing, 135–36

Career goals, 51–52, 85–86, 91, 115, 131–32, 157–58
Clutter, eliminating, 25–26
Cognitive Therapy, 91–92
Collective healing, 147–48, 177
Colorism, eliminating, 16, 187–88
Comfort zone, 29–30, 47–48, 113–14, 125–26, 137–38, 147–48, 177–78
Communication
  ancestors and, 77–78
  assertive communication, 77–78
  of feelings, 137–38
  tips for, 13–14, 35–36, 77–80, 137–38
  XYZ method for, 77–78

Community
  building, 75–76
  caring for, 12
  existing in, 147–48
  healing in, 11–12, 147–48
  investing in, 163–64, 205–6
  participating in, 163–64, 205–6
  racism in, 205–6
  resilience of, 149–50
  strengthening, 197–98, 205–6
Cooper, Christian, 129–30
Coping skills
  active coping plan, 11, 109–10,
    199–200
  for depression, 17–18, 69–70, 129–30
  healthy coping routine, 133–34
  for stress, 29–30, 109–10
  for trauma, 12, 21–22, 53–54, 69–70,
    191–92, 209–12
COVID-19, 25, 97, 106, 165, 206
Cruz, Kleaver, 211
Crying, space for, 65–66
Cultural programming, 12, 33–34,
  75–76

Dance therapy, 177–78
Dates, with others, 188
Dates, with self, 125–26
Decision-making tips, 155–56
Decluttering tips, 25–26
Depression
  assessing, 61–62, 69–70
  coping with, 17–18, 69–70, 129–30
  screening for, 62, 69–70
  social media and, 174
  therapy for, 17–18
*Diagnostic and Statistical Manual of
  Mental Disorders*, 189
Dialectal Behavioral Therapy (DBT), 156
Diet, 29–30, 33–34, 207–8
Doctor appointments, 31–32

Donaghue, Chris, 183
Dreams, revisiting, 115–16
DuBois, W.E.B., 89

Emotions/feelings
  conceptualizing, 133–34
  embracing, 45–46, 65–66, 113–14,
    151–56, 175–76, 211–12
  expressing, 13–14, 41–46, 57–58,
    65–66, 79–80, 95–100, 119–20,
    127–28, 137–38, 169–70, 209–12
  processing, 13–14, 53–54, 59–62,
    87–88, 95–96, 101–2, 109–10, 127–
    28, 141–42, 145–46, 153–54, 161–62
Energy level
  assessing, 29–30, 71–73
  checking, 81–82
  hope and, 151–52
  increasing, 29–30, 135–36, 177–78,
    199–200
  monitoring, 81–82
Environment, personalizing, 179–80
Exercise, benefits of, 11, 23–24, 39–40,
  177–78, 199–200

Father wound, healing, 117–18
Finances, handling, 197–98
Float therapy, 43–44
Foods, 29–30, 33–34, 207–8
Forest bathing, 129–30
Forgiveness, 95–96
Frankl, Viktor, 121
Friendships, 12, 56, 97–98, 103–4, 125–27

Garner, Eric, 21
Garza, Alicia, 76
G.L.A.D. technique, 67–68
Goals
  for career, 51–52, 85–86, 91, 115,
    131–32, 157–58
  focus on, 29–30, 85–86, 107–8, 132, 170

racism and, 131
setting, 85–86, 107–8, 131–32, 170
SMART goals, 107–8, 132, 170
Gratitude, practicing, 67–68
Grief, acknowledging, 127–28, 161, 167
Grooming habits, 93–94
Gutierrez, Natalie, 150, 213

"Harlem," 115
Healing. *See also* Therapy
collective healing, 147–48, 177
in community, 11–12, 147–48
dance and, 177–78
of father wound, 117–18
holistic healing, 29–30
of mother wound, 12, 171–72
power of, 147–48
of relationships, 12, 117–18, 171–72
of trauma, 153–54, 171–72, 177–78,
209–12
Help, asking for, 63–64, 191–92
Heritage, 175–76. *See also* Ancestors
Hersey, Tricia, 111
Highs/lows, reflecting on, 79–80
Holistic healing, 29–30
Holocaust, 53, 121
Home, personalizing, 179–80
Home sanctuary, 11, 27–28
hooks, bell, 97, 213–14
Hope
cultivating, 131, 151–52
dreams and, 115–16
power of, 151–52
radical hope, 131, 151–52
sense of, 175–76
Hughes, Langston, 115
Hygiene, daily, 83–84, 93–94

"I" statements, 78, 138
Impostor syndrome, 51–52, 157–58
Inner child, 153–54, 212

Intentions, setting, 85–86, 119
Isolation, 15–16, 97–98, 109–10, 137–
38, 147–48, 165, 193, 205

Jim Crow, 53, 111, 139
Johnson, George M., 214
Journaling, 13–14, 41–46, 66, 96,
119–20, 152, 170, 210
Joy, embracing, 11, 211–12
Jung, Carl, 119

Kid Cudi, 61
King, Martin Luther King Jr., 149

Letters, writing, 35–36, 128
LGBTQIA+ family, 75–76, 206
Liberation, 63–66, 75–78, 141–52,
163–64, 175–76, 187–92, 205–6
Lil Wayne, 61
Loneliness, 97–98, 109–10, 147–48,
173–74. *See also* Isolation

Macaroni Union, 161
Man's Search for Meaning, 121
Massage therapy, 165–66
Matrix, The, 134
Meals, preparing, 33–34, 207–8
Meaning-making, 121–22, 164, 167, 195
Media messages, 173–74, 203–4
Medical appointments, 31–32
Meditation
benefits of, 27–28, 47–48, 101–2, 119,
129
for connecting with ancestors, 150
forest bathing and, 129
intentional work and, 119
mindfulness and, 145–46
practicing, 47–48, 101–2
sanctuary for, 27–28
Mental health. *See also* Therapy

assessing, 11–12, 61–62, 173–74,
189–90
improving, 19–20, 135–36, 189–90
racism and, 61–62
workplace and, 61–62, 135–36, 190
Mental health day, 135–36
Mental illness, 23, 26, 61, 189–90
Microaggression, 99–100
Mind-body connection, 23, 30, 199–200
Mindfulness, 39–40, 129–30, 139–46,
169–70, 207–8. *See also* Meditation
Minority stress, 37
"Monkey mind," 39, 102
Mother wound, healing, 12, 171–72
Movement therapy, 177–78, 199–200
Music therapy, 161–62, 195–96

Naps, taking, 111–12
National Museum of African American
History and Culture, 212
Nature, enjoying, 39–40, 48, 129–30,
160
Negative thoughts, 91–92, 109–10
Nutrition, 29–30, 33–34, 207–8

Obituary, writing, 167–68
Organization tips, 19–20, 25–26

*Pain We Carry: Healing from Complex
PTSD for People of Color*, 150, 213
Pandemic, 25, 97, 106, 165, 206
Parks, enjoying, 39–40, 129–30, 160,
212
Parks, Rosa, 149
Peace, finding, 11, 21–22, 26–30,
57–58, 119–20, 193–98, 210–12
Perspective, changing, 15–16, 27–30,
67–68, 87–90, 145–56, 167–76
Pets, time with, 139–40
Playlist, positive, 161–62
Poetry, writing, 212

Positive qualities, 185–86
Positive thoughts, 67–68, 91–92,
161–62
Prayer, 48, 128, 150, 152
Prejudice, 73–74, 98, 159, 165, 187–88,
205
Project Implicit, 188

Qualities, positive, 185–86
Quiet time, 27–28, 55–56, 86, 123–26,
129–30, 135–36, 182

Racial pride, 175–76
Racial trauma, 12, 21, 141–42, 162,
193–94, 199. *See also* Trauma
Racism
anti-Black racism, 124, 141–42
barriers of, 115–16, 131–32
burden of, 53–54
career and, 51–52, 157–58
colorism and, 16, 187–88
in community, 205–6
countering, 73–74
discussions about, 149–50
experiences with, 141–42
family and, 209–10
goals and, 131
mental health and, 61–62
safe space and, 159–60
workplace and, 29, 51–52, 61–62, 157–58
Radical acceptance, 11, 193–94
Radical hope, 131, 151–52
Rage, handling, 57–58, 128, 211–12
Reading habits, 89–90, 143–44
Refuge, 11, 27–28. *See also* Safe spaces
Relationships
building, 12, 75–76
friendships, 12, 56, 97–98, 103–4,
125–27
healing, 12, 117–18, 171–72

romantic relationships, 13, 56, 98, 127, 188

Religious practices, 47–48, 151–52, 163–64

Resilience, 63–64, 114, 121–22, 149–50, 163, 195

Resistance, 73–74, 111, 211–12

Rest, quality of, 83–84, 87–88, 111–12, 199

Romance, 13, 56, 98, 127, 188

Roses & Thorns technique, 79–80

Rustin, Bayard, 76

Safe spaces
confidential spaces, 181–82
creating, 60, 182
finding, 17, 60, 129–30, 159–60, 174, 181–82, 195
music and, 195–96
racism and, 159–60

Sanctuary, creating, 11, 27–28

Sanders, Joshunda, 139

"Say It Loud: I'm Black and I'm Proud," 187

Screening tools, 62, 69–70

Self-acceptance, 11, 193–94

Self-care. *See also specific activities*
benefits of, 11–14, 29–30
importance of, 11–12, 29–32, 37–38
process of, 13–14, 29–30

Self-compassion, 119, 182

Self-confidence, 181–84

Self-definition, 12, 15–16, 63–64, 149–50, 175–76

Self-determination, 12, 85–86, 169–70

Self-esteem, 91, 181–84

Self-forgiveness, 95–96

Self-help, 89–90, 143–44, 151–54, 185

Self-love, 211–12

Self-reflection, 13–14, 37–60, 79–80, 86, 95–96, 101–2, 141–42

Sensitivity, 59–60, 113–14. *See also* Emotions/feelings

Sensory deprivation, 43–44

Sexual dysfunction, 183–84

Sexual health, 71–72, 183–84, 201–2

Shadow work, 119–20

Shadow Work Workbook, The, 120

Shame, releasing, 45–46, 95–96, 209–10

Simpson, O. J., 16

Sims, James Marion, 31

Sleep routine, 83–84, 87–88

SMART goals, 107–8, 132, 170. *See also* Goals

Social justice, 75–77, 111, 115, 127, 159, 201, 205–6

Social media, limiting, 173–74, 203–4

Softness, embracing, 113–14

Songs, 77, 161–62, 177–78, 187, 195–96, 212. *See also* Music therapy

Soul food, 33–34, 207–8

Spiritual guides, 149–50

Spiritual health, 11–12, 47–48, 163–64

Spiritual practice, 47–48, 150–52, 163–64

Stop Woke Act, 149

Storytelling, 141–42, 177

Strength, redefining, 63–64

Stress. *See also* Anxieties; Trauma
coping with, 29–30, 109–10
managing, 19–20, 25–26, 29–30, 37–38, 61–62, 157–58, 189–90, 203–4
minority stress, 37
racial stress, 12, 21, 141–42, 162, 193–94, 199
reducing, 27–28, 39–40, 53–54, 123–24, 135–46, 161–62, 165–66, 199–200
screening tools for, 62, 69–70
worry dumps for, 87–88

Stretches, 23–24

Talk therapy, 17–18
Therapy. *See also* Healing
  behavioral therapy, 156
  benefits of, 17–18, 43–44, 91–92, 156,
    161–62, 177–78, 195–96
  cognitive therapy, 91–92
  dance therapy, 177–78
  float therapy, 43–44
  massage therapy, 165–66
  mental health and, 189–90
  movement therapy, 177–78, 199–200
  music therapy, 161–62, 195–96
  pets and, 139–40
  psychotherapy, 17–18
  safe spaces and, 17, 181–82
  talk therapy, 17–18
  therapy dogs, 140
Till, Emmett, 201
Time for self, 27–28, 55–56, 86, 123–
  26, 129–30, 135–36, 182
To-do lists, 11, 19–20, 108
Toxic behaviors, 55–56, 169
Traditions, 68, 150, 164, 177–78, 207
Trauma. *See also* Anxieties; Stress
  coping with, 12, 21–22, 53–54, 69–70,
    191–92, 209–12
  healing, 153–54, 171–72, 177–78,
    209–12
  intergenerational trauma, 16, 34, 59,
    111–12, 209–10
  racial trauma, 12, 21, 141–42, 162,
    193–94, 199
  vicarious trauma, 21, 53–54
Trips, taking, 123–24
Tuskegee Experiment, 31, 61
Twitter, 173

Values, clarifying, 12, 169–70
Vision boards, 131–32
Vulnerabilities
  embracing, 32, 45–46, 65–66, 113–14

  inner child and, 153–54
  reflecting on, 13–14, 79–80
  social media and, 173–74
  weaknesses, 17, 59–60, 181–82

Walks, enjoying, 39–40, 125, 129, 145,
  208
Washington, Booker T., 89
Weaknesses, 17, 59–60, 181–82. *See also*
  Vulnerabilities
"Weightless," 161
Weightlessness, 44, 161, 192
*We Real Cool: Black Men and Masculin-
  ity*, 97, 213
White mediocrity, 157–58
*Will to Change: Men, Masculinity, and
  Love*, 214
Wise Mind strategy, 155–56
Workplace
  career goals, 51–52, 85–86, 91, 115,
    131–32, 157–58
  mental health and, 61–62, 135–36, 190
  organizing, 25–26
  personalizing, 179–80
  racism and, 29, 51–52, 61–62, 157–58
  time away from, 135–36
Worry dumps, 87–88
Wounds, healing, 12, 117–18, 171–72
Writing exercises
  journaling, 13–14, 41–46, 66, 96,
    119–20, 152, 170, 210
  letter writing, 35–36, 128
  obituary, 167–68
  poems/lyrics, 212
  writing tips, 13–16, 67–68, 87–88,
    142, 186

XYZ method, 77–78

Yoga, 23, 27, 29
YouTube, 208

About the Author

Jor-El Caraballo, LMHC, is a licensed therapist and cofounder of Viva, a multi-state mental health practice. Caraballo received a BA in psychology from the University of North Carolina at Wilmington, and MA and EdM degrees in psychological counseling from Teachers College, Columbia University. He has been featured as a mental health expert across many magazines and websites, including *mindbodygreen*, *Men's Health*, *Healthline*, *Insider*, *Self*, and more, sharing advice and insight on self-care, interpersonal relationships, dealing with trauma, and more.